REVIVAL
THE NEW TESTAMENT EXPECTATION

REVIVAL
THE NEW TESTAMENT EXPECTATION

Is there a New Testament Theology of Revival?

JONATHAN F. BAYES

RESOURCE *Publications* · Eugene, Oregon

REVIVAL: THE NEW TESTAMENT EXPECTATION
Is there a New Testament Theology of Revival?

Resource Publications
An Imprint of Wipf and Stock Publishers
199 W. 8th Ave., Suite 3
Eugene, OR 97401

www.wipfandstock.com

ISBN 13: 978-1-4982-3526-6

Manufactured in the U.S.A.   01/06/2016

All Scripture citations are from the New King James Version of the Bible © 1982 by Thomas Nelson, Inc., Nashville, Tenessee.

CONTENTS

1 **A New Testament Theology of Revival?** | 1

2 **The Teaching on Revival in the Gospels** | 5

3 **The Teaching on Revival in the Book of Acts** | 60

4 **The Teaching on Revival in the New Testament Letters** | 94

5 **The Teaching on Revival in the Book of Revelation** | 119

6 **Conclusion: Revival a New Testament Theme** | 140

7 **Postscript:** *Rise Up, You Heirs of God's Salvation* | 143

Bibliography | 145
Scripture Index | 147

1

A NEW TESTAMENT THEOLOGY
OF REVIVAL?

The theme of revival has been brought forcibly to my attention lately. At the time of writing I have been involved for several years in a movement of prayer for revival amongst the Bible-believing churches of Yorkshire in the north of England. It started at the beginning of 2011, when the Yorkshire Reformed Ministers' Fraternal issued a call to prayer addressed to the churches of Yorkshire. An invitation was given to a united prayer gathering, to be held in Leeds for two hours one Saturday morning in March of that year. The stated purpose was to cry out to God to revive our love for Jesus, and to pour out his Spirit so that the work of the gospel will advance in power across our region, in our nation as a whole, and throughout the entire world.

This came about as a result of a memorable meeting of the Fraternal in December, 2010. At that meeting it became apparent that the pastors were growing increasingly burdened by the obvious fact that we are living in dark and desperate days. The work of the gospel seems largely to have stagnated, and the tide of unbelief and immorality rushes in. One brother after another voiced this burden and frustration. And together we recognized that our only hope is in God, that we cannot turn the tide. Only an outpouring of the Holy Spirit will enable the gospel to advance with power, and the churches to grow.

The response to that initial gathering in March, 2011, was truly encouraging. About a hundred and twenty people gathered, representing over twenty different churches, from all over Yorkshire. This convinced us that we should continue to meet regularly to pray for revival, and an ongoing Concert of Prayer for revival is now underway. We have met at roughly quarterly intervals. Sometimes we meet at a venue to which people travel from all over the county. More often we meet in a network of smaller meetings at various venues around the county. The numbers participating have increased, and often about two hundred people, from over fifty congregations, have assembled to cry out to the Lord for the necessary visitation from on high.

What has been especially heartening is the fact that around the country a number of other people have been motivated by what has happened in Yorkshire to call the churches of their own areas to prayer. Since the beginning of 2012 further prayer meetings have been held in other parts of the country, deliberately timed to coincide with the gatherings in Yorkshire. Meetings have taken place, to our knowledge, from Devon in the south to Edinburgh in the north. People all over the country share the same burden to see the Lord at work in our midst in mighty power in this generation for the glory of his name.

However, after the first united gathering for prayer for revival in March 2011, I received an email from a brother minister who raised a few questions about the practice of holding a concert of prayer for revival. Amongst his comments was one which pointed out how so much of the biblical support for the idea of praying for revival is taken from the Old Testament. He wondered whether the New Testament would encourage prayer for revival, and, if so, how.

This struck me as a valid concern. It is indeed very often the Old Testament promises and prophecies which are used to undergird our longing and expectancy for revival. Is this because the New Testament has nothing to say on this theme? I found that hard to believe, so I set myself the task of trying to discover what basis there is in the New Testament for a theology of revival. This book is the result.

My approach was to travel through the books of the New Testament more or less in canonical order, and so gradually to build up a picture of what the New Testament says about this theme.

It is, of course, true that the word "revival" and its cognates are not found in the New Testament in relevant contexts.[1] These terms do occur

---

1. The word "revived" does appear at Rom 7:9, but it is talking about the reviving of sin.

in the Old Testament, on twenty occasions in the New King James Version where the context is relevant to this subject.[2] However, the Greek terms chosen by the Septuagint translators are not used in the New Testament in places where the context is relevant to the theme of revival.[3] This meant that I could not simply do a word study. Rather, I had to look at passages where the theme of revival is implicit, even though the specific word may not be explicitly used.

Furthermore, the word "revival" suggests to some people a harking back to some mythical "good old days," and wanting to see what has happened in the past replicated in our time. That is not the way in which the word has typically been used theologically. However, if the word becomes a stumbling-block, then it is better to find an alternative term. Since "revival" is not a New Testament word, we do not need to get hung up on the specific term. What we call what we are praying for is neither here nor there. It's the reality that matters—and the reality which we long for is a mighty outpouring of the Holy Spirit leading to the rekindling of love for Christ on the part of his people, and an explosion of gospel effectiveness with a visible impact on the nation and the world. Is this something which the New Testament gives us the right to expect?

I am now inviting you to accompany me on this voyage of discovery. The conclusion to which we shall gradually come is that there is a very clear and definite New Testament theology of revival, which must be set in the context of the Father's promises to his Son, recorded in the Old Testament. The New Testament, it seems to me, encourages us to expect the steady, unfolding fulfillment of these promises in the course of this gospel age, such that, if ever we live through a period in any place, where gospel progress is not apparent, where the life of the church does not match up to the New Testament ideal, then we are compelled to see that as an aberration. At such times, and in such places, we ought to be crying out earnestly to God to revive his work in the midst of the years.

However, our danger is that we come to think that the current state of affairs is normal. We have lost our proper expectancy. We tend to explain away the promises in the light of our experience, instead of letting

---

2. Ezra 9:8–9; Pss 71:20; 80:18; 85:6; 119:25, 37, 40, 88, 107, 149, 154, 156, 159; 138:7; 143:11; Isa 57:15 (x2); Hos 14:7; Hab 3:2.

3. Four different Greek words are used, all of which are cognates of *zōē*, meaning "life."

God's promises shape our expectations and our prayers. We have become despondent, where we should be bursting with hope.

But all that is to anticipate. Let's start our journey through the pages of the New Testament.

2

THE TEACHING ON REVIVAL
IN THE GOSPELS

MATTHEW 1:1

To look for a New Testament theology of revival cannot mean that we ignore the Old Testament. The New Testament is deeply rooted in the Old. The Old Testament is the shadow of which the New is the reality. When the risen Lord was speaking to the pair on the road to Emmaus, "beginning at Moses and all the prophets, he expounded to them in all the Scriptures the things concerning himself" (Luke 24:27). The very first verse of the New Testament establishes this inextricable link with the Old Testament. It forces us immediately to find the promises of revival which the Old Testament holds out, and to set them in the context of the total purpose of God spanning both Testaments, and uniting all the separate eras of time and history in a single divine program. It is in the light of what God has done with the coming of Jesus Christ into the world that the full meaning of the Old Testament is finally illuminated. The New Testament thus pulls the Old Testament hope into its own theology of revival.

In the opening verse of the New Testament, Jesus Christ is described as "the son of David, the son of Abraham." These two epithets take us into a wealth of Old Testament prophecy which is relevant to, and, indeed, foundational for, a New Testament theology of revival.[1]

Son of David

The phrase "son of David" takes up the promise which the LORD made to David in 1 Chronicles 17:11–14. The LORD promised that the throne of a son of David would be established for ever. Matthew 1:1 insists that it is in Jesus Christ that this promise finds its ultimate fulfillment.

Building on that first prophecy to David, there are many Old Testament passages which indicate what conditions will be like when the kingdom is indeed established in the hands of this son of David. They too are part of the Old Testament background presupposed as the New Testament opens.

Psalms

We turn first to the book of Psalms. There are three Psalms which we shall look at.

PSALM 89

This Psalm is a direct meditation on the promise to David. It describes that promise as a covenant. That means that it is a solemn declaration which the LORD guarantees to fulfill. He himself assumes all the obligations for securing its fulfillment.

The Psalm begins with praise to the LORD for his sovereign rule over creation. Then from verse 15 it begins to describe the blessedness of those who experience the joyful reality of living under God's sovereign reign. It then continues by showing how that sovereign reign of God has been brought down to earth in the person of the king descended from David. In him God's power will be established. His foes will collapse before his advance. The power of Christ will be seen across the seas. He will be the highest of the kings of the earth, not just theoretically, but in the actual conditions of life in this world, with all its political structures.

---

1. Luke's infancy narratives make the same connection with David (Luke 1:32–33; 2:4, 11) and Abraham (Luke 1:55, 73).

Verses 30–45 admit that, at the time when this Psalm was written, the covenant with David appeared to have stalled. The kings of Judah, descended from David, had not lived in obedience to the law of the LORD. Consequently, God's people had been overpowered by their enemies, and the Davidic line of descent had come to an end. However, the Psalm ends with prayer. The Psalmist cries out to the LORD for a reversal of the present distress.

Perhaps it is true to say that, in the circumstances of those days, we see a paradigm of days like our own, when gospel progress is not uniform in all nations, because our sin has resulted in David's honorable Son not getting the glory he deserves in our nation, and from our leaders. This Psalm is therefore our mandate to pray for the revival of the kingdom, for the quickening of the preaching of the gospel, here, now, in our time and place, so that our nation may again know the blessedness of the joyful sound of God's sovereign rule in his Son through the message of grace; that our leaders may again understand that Jesus Christ is the highest of the kings of the earth, and may submit to his rule in obedience to the law of God, and so set the example which will lead the people to follow Jesus and live in the joy of the gospel.

It is possible that we might interpret this Psalm, and, indeed, all the Old Testament prophecies, in two ways which lessen their relevance to prayer for revival. The glorious promises here might be relegated to the eternal future, and not be read as God's pledge to give his beloved Son the victory through the preaching of the gospel in the present age. However, there are several allusions in the Psalm which point to a reference to this gospel era, which continues from Pentecost to the Lord's second coming. The whole context is one of expectancy that this covenant will be fulfilled in our history, and frustration that it has not yet been fulfilled completely. Moreover, verses 22–23 fix the Psalm as a prophecy of a day and age when Christ's enemies are still around, but have been rendered totally powerless. That cannot be a reference to heaven. By then, they will exist no more.

Alternatively, the whole Psalm might be spiritualized so that its fulfillment is seen as the rule of Christ in the hearts of those individuals who are saved by his grace through the gospel. However, this would make the prayer at the end of the Psalm totally misplaced. The Psalmist is not there praying that the LORD will after all save him. He utters these words out of a total confidence that God has already shown mercy to him personally. What he longs for is the public, visible, obvious manifestation of the glory of Christ throughout the world. His concern is the reproach which Christ faces in a world where his enemies seem to have gained the upper hand. And so we are called to join in the same cry in our day that the LORD's loving kindnesses to his Son may be renewed in a massive outpouring of gospel blessing.

PSALM 72

We turn back a few pages to a Psalm which was written by Solomon. He was the initial fulfillment of God's promise to David of a son who would sit on his throne. However, Solomon himself, inspired by the Holy Spirit, recognizes that the true fulfillment must go far beyond anything which is realized in his own life and times. He envisages an era of justice and peace, a time when oppressive regimes will be a thing of the past, a time when the world's peoples will, without exception, be lavishly provided for: famine, too, will be a thing of the past. This state of affairs will continue for generations—in fact, for as the long as the sun continues to shine in the sky, as the generality of humankind will fear the LORD. Moreover, Solomon is quite clear that the kingdom of "great David's greater Son" will be universal in its extent. All the nations and their rulers will acknowledge the higher throne to which they must bow, all the enemies of the gospel will be subdued, and all the world's peoples shall truly flourish under God's rich blessing.

In the middle of the Psalm we find an interesting phrase in verse 15. It says that continual prayer will be made for the king. It may seem a strange idea that we should pray for Jesus. We are more accustomed to thinking of him as the one to whom we pray, rather than one for whom we pray. However, this shows that constant prayer that the kingdom of Jesus will indeed flourish in this world is a proper part of Christian spirituality and church life. Verse 18 stresses the point that only the LORD can do such wondrous things as to establish the kingdom of Christ unfalteringly in this world. So we must pray that he will do so.

Once again this Psalm could be interpreted as speaking either of the eternal future, or of Christ's spiritual kingdom in the hearts of believers. However, there are indications here also that the Psalm is about Christ's public reign in this present age, the gospel era. We are told that these prophecies relate to the period during which the sun and the moon continue to shine. In other words they are for us to embrace now, not merely to hope for in a remote and distant future. Again, if the Psalm is spiritualized to speak of the individual salvation of people from every nation, though not of a victory of Christ affecting the nations as such, this would make the final cry of the Psalm rather disappointing. Solomon foresees a day when the whole earth will be filled with the glory of Christ. It is true that that glory is displayed in the conversion and salvation of those for whom he died. But if there is never to be a day when the fruits of his atonement and resurrection are seen in the conversion of massive numbers of sinners from every corner of the globe, then it is hard to see how the Psalm can really be prophesying a day when the whole earth will be filled with that glory. Such an interpretation reduces that vision to mean that parts of the earth will have a little bit of glory here and there. But the inspired writer seems, surely, to envisage something far greater than that, something far more glorious, something far more God-honoring, something far more fitting to the splendors of Christ's person. And we are invited to devote ourselves to continuous prayer for Jesus' honor in this world right now.

PSALM 132

This Psalm begins with a reference to David's afflictions. He was afflicted in soul at the lack of a suitable dwelling place for the Mighty God. He committed himself to secure an appropriate place. We know, of course, that the task of building the temple fell to Solomon. Nevertheless, in the latter period of his reign, David made extensive preparations. Here we see an Old Testament picture of Jesus Christ, the one who was afflicted on the cross in order to bring to reality the people who would be the dwelling place of God for all eternity.

And the Psalm looks forward to the fulfillment of God's promise to David that his descendant would sit on his throne for evermore. Zion, another picture, fulfilled in the worldwide gathering of believers into the congregation of Christ, will be God's resting place. We are perhaps familiar with the saying that "our hearts are restless until we find our rest in God." It is equally, and even more amazingly, true that God's heart is restless until he finds his rest in us. And that was the purpose of Christ's coming as the Son of David—to enable God's heart to be at rest. But the people in whom God finds his rest are abundantly provided for, satisfied, saved, filled with joy. And David's kingdom, finally realized in Jesus Christ, will grow as his enemies are put to shame, and his crown flourishes.

So there we see what we should be expecting now, here, in this gospel age, in our setting: that Christ's kingdom will be growing and flourishing. Because that is what God says that he will do. Is that happening? Well, yes, in some places, but surely not here just now. Shouldn't that drive us to cry out, "Lord, then do it." How can we be satisfied with anything less than a growing church, a flourishing kingdom, a Christ who is getting the honor he deserves in our nation today?

The Prophets: Jeremiah

In addition to these Psalms there are passages in the prophets which take up God's promise to David in 1 Chronicles 17. We shall just glance at Jeremiah as an example.

In both Jeremiah 23:5 and 33:15 the prophet is looking forward to coming days when the LORD will raise up to David a Branch of righteousness. This is defined as a King whose reign is prosperous, and who executes judgment and righteousness in the earth. This pair of terms speaks of sound teaching accompanied by, and leading to, right action. Jeremiah 33:17 looks forward to the endless establishment of David's kingdom, and in verses 20–26 the prophet makes the link with the covenant promise, which is as unbreakable as the Creator's covenant with his creation. This is the promise which Matthew 1:1 tells us is fulfilled in Jesus Christ.

Once again, we notice that the prophet is not looking to the eternal future, but to future days on earth, and that he is not referring to a spiritual kingdom in the hearts of individual believers, but to life in the earth, to a kingdom which is visible, obvious, and successful. Certainly the starting point is personal salvation, because it is the fact that the LORD is himself our righteousness which is the foundation for life in his kingdom. It is instructive to observe the slight difference between 23:6 and 33:16. In the earlier passage "The LORD our righteousness" is the title by which the LORD himself is known. In chapter 33 the same title is ascribed to the LORD's people symbolized by the city of Jerusalem. This emphasizes the intimate unity between Christ and his people, and their total dependence on him for their righteous standing in his sight.

In the first instance these passages speak of the gathering to Christ of the people of Israel out of all the countries where they live. However, chapter 33 sets this great hope in a larger context. It speaks in greater detail of the nature of the kingdom which Jesus will establish in the world. Health will flourish. Peace will be abundant. Joyful song and fervent praise will be the dominant notes in this kingdom, and the root of these blessings will be the cleansing and forgiveness of sin. But in verse 9, Jeremiah turns his eyes outwards to the Gentile nations of the world. There is a day coming when the kingdom of Christ will be "a name of joy, a praise, and an honor before all the nations of the earth." The prophet foresees how the nations will hear of the good which God has done for his people, of the prosperity which he has given them, with the result that they too will fear and tremble before the LORD. I think Calvin is right to read this as a description of the conversion of the Gentile nations.[2] Jeremiah recognizes that God's great work amongst the Jews in the person of Christ will result in the worldwide outflow of grace and salvation, so that Gentile nations as such become obedient to God. That is what revival entails. It is when national life is transformed by the mighty impact of the gospel of grace proclaimed in the power of the Holy Spirit. It is what we must expect in the light of Matthew 1:1 and its reference back to Old Testament promises. The reference to David in the opening verse of the New Testament surely gives us a warrant to pray for worldwide and national revival.

Son of Abraham

The other connection with the Old Testament which Matthew 1:1 makes is to Genesis 12. Jesus Christ is the "son of Abraham," so the covenant promise to Abraham finds its ultimate fulfillment in him. The heart of God's promise to Abraham is the blessing of the world. In Genesis 12:1–3, the word "blessing," or a cognate, is used five times. God promises to bless Abraham, but this is not an exclusive blessing to be enjoyed by Abraham and his descendants alone. God promises that Abraham will be a blessing, and what that means is defined in the final phrase of verse 3: in Abraham all the families of the earth shall be blessed. This promise is repeated in slightly different words in Genesis 18:18, where the LORD confirms that all nations will be blessed in Abraham, and the method of its fulfillment is made more explicit in Genesis 22:18, where the LORD says to Abraham, "in your seed all the nations of the earth shall be blessed." The fulfillment will take place not in the person of Abraham himself, but in one who is designated his seed, that is to say, in Jesus Christ, the true son of Abraham. The LORD repeats the promise in exactly the same terms to Isaac in Genesis 26:4, and

2. Calvin, *Jeremiah and Lamentations*, Vol. 4, 240–41.

in Genesis 28:14 he passes on the promise to Jacob, reverting now to the word "families."

So God's ancient purpose was eventually to bless all the nations of the world in Christ. And we must ask, what is it for a nation to be blessed? We find the answer in Psalm 33:12. It is when the LORD, the true God, the God who has made himself known in his Son Jesus Christ, is a nation's God, that the nation is blessed. In other words, it is when the Gospel makes such an impact that widespread conversions are recorded, when true revival takes place in a nation, that there is true blessing. That should be the major burden of our praying, because as the next line of this verse makes clear, such a wonderful state of affairs is in the sovereign power of God alone.

The alternation between the words "nations" and "families" in the Genesis texts emphasizes two things. First, it is nations, not merely individuals, that God intends to bless. The kingdom of Jesus is not merely set up in individual hearts. It is also a public, visible phenomenon, which makes an impact on nations as nations. Isaiah 19:24–25 looks forward to the day when that is fulfilled, when the nations of Egypt and Assyria are blessed along with Israel. Let's pray that the recent upheavals in the Middle East might prove to be the start of the fulfillment of this prophecy. Second, this impact is truly as widespread as could be. It is all the families in all the nations which are to be blessed—not just a few families in a few nations, not even a few families in all nations—but every family in every nation is to be brought into the blessing of living under the reign of Christ in this world. Here is a great hope. Here is something which we must regularly pray to be realized.

We have been looking in some detail at Old Testament passages. Are these really appropriate in a New Testament theology of revival? Yes they are. The opening verse of the New Testament ties that section of God's word inextricably to the former section. Matthew 1:1 indicates that these Old Testament prophecies are fulfilled in Jesus Christ. As a result, they have to be drawn in to become part of a New Testament theology of revival. As we continue, we shall see that the New Testament does this repeatedly.

THE MINISTRY OF JOHN THE BAPTIST

It is not only the opening verse of the New Testament which forms a bridge back to the Old Testament. Many times the New Testament cites Old Testament passages which contain Messianic promises, which are therefore drawn into a New Testament theology of revival. This is evident in the narratives of John the Baptist's ministry.

Old Testament Quotations

The Gospel writers refer to two passages in particular as fulfilled in the ministry of John the Baptist.

Isaiah 40:3–8

Isaiah 40:3 is quoted in Matthew 3:3, Mark 1:3, and John 1:23. John is a voice crying in the wilderness, whose purpose is to prepare the way of the LORD. The LORD is about to come, and John's ministry is one of preparation. The words quoted are the opening verse of a stanza (Isaiah 40:3–5) which goes on to depict the LORD's steady progress. Luke quotes the entire stanza (Luke 3:4–6). Every obstacle will be overcome as the LORD advances through the world. As a result of his coming, the present wilderness will be replaced by a vision of glory which will be seen by all the world. Luke replaces these words by the phrase which follows them in the Septuagint translation of Isaiah 9:5: "All flesh shall see the salvation of God." God's glory is seen most splendidly in the salvation which he provides in Christ, and it is to be seen absolutely everywhere.

Isaiah then goes on in verses 6–8 to emphasize the point that we must not assess God's word in the light of the fluctuating circumstances of human experience. It is true that we observe situations which flourish for a while and then wither. Even in Christian experience this is true. There are ups and downs in the fortunes of churches. Specific congregations experience cycles of growth and decline. The wider church in a particular region or nation may go through periods of stagnation. At such times we can easily become pessimistic, even despairing. We conclude that the gospel is never going to conquer the globe. We anticipate ongoing decline, and start assuming that only the second coming of Christ will save the day. But this is to subject the promises of God's word to our experience, to judge the word of God by the circumstances which we observe. And that is basically the approach of liberal theology. Isaiah 6:8 tells us that "the word of our God stands forever," so we must hold on to the word of promise, and cry urgently to the LORD that he will fulfil his stated purpose, clear away the obstacles, and hasten the time when all flesh shall see the glory of the LORD.

I understand that to be a promise that the glory of God in the face of Jesus Christ will be universally seen through the preaching of the gospel. The LORD has now come in Christ, but his incarnation and his baptism were just the beginning, as Mark 1:1 indicates. We should now expect the steady progress of the gospel, until, through the preaching of the message, all flesh truly sees the glory of God in his work of salvation. Moreover, this is not a vision at a distance, or a vision which is a mere matter of intellectual curiosity. This is a life-changing vision. This is a vision which results in conversion and discipleship. If at any time we are not seeing the gospel overcoming all obstacles and people being converted in great numbers, then we must be driven to our knees, pleading the promises which must stand forever.

Malachi 3–4

In Mark's Gospel the quotation from Isaiah 40:3 is prefaced by another quotation, from Malachi 3:1 (Mark 1:2): "Behold, I send my messenger before your face, who will prepare your way before you." Later, addressing the crowds after he had finished speaking with some messengers sent by John the Baptist, Jesus would confirm these words as fulfilled in John's ministry (Matthew 11:10). Malachi 3 anticipates God coming to refine his people, resulting in overflowing blessing observed by all nations. Chapter 4 then foresees the victory of the righteous, and sees John the Baptist's ministry as playing a pivotal role in the reunification of the world to avert its destruction. This is what Jesus has achieved as he builds on the work of his forerunner. We must therefore pray earnestly for this promised day of overflowing blessing for the people of Israel, and for the reunification of all nations and all generations as one people in Christ.

A Picture of Revival

John the Baptist's ministry was evidently very effective. Matthew 3:5 (cf. Mark 1:5) tells us of great numbers coming to hear him from every district of the region where he was baptizing. This has been described as "the first discernible revival in the New Testament."[3] Whether this is a valid description or not depends on our precise understanding of revival. I prefer to

---

3. Cauchi, *Revivals*, line 16.

reserve the word "revival" for the clear fulfillment of the Messianic promises. If we use the term more generally of any large scale spiritual work, we risk missing the essential Christ-centeredness of revival. Revival can then become an end in itself, and we can almost make an idol out of big numbers and successful churches. However, if we see revival as the Father's fulfillment of his promises to his Son, then Christ retains his proper central place in our concerns. In that case I would see John the Baptist's ministry more as a preview or a picture of revival, perhaps as a proto-revival, than as a revival in its own right.

As a picture of revival, there are two features of John the Baptist's ministry which are typical elements of any real revival, two aspects which will always be replicated where the Father is fulfilling his promises to his Son.

A Huge Impact

First, God's word made a huge impact on an entire area, and on large numbers of people. Men and women flocked to hear the word of God. That will always happen in a revival.

The First Impact

Second, the first impact of God's word was confession of sin and repentance (Matthew 3:6; Mark 1:4; Luke 3:3). There is not much of a sense of sin in the land today. The prevalent view is that everything is merely a matter of opinion. School teachers refuse to tell children the difference between right and wrong. Indeed, they seem to find a sinister pleasure in undermining the very concept of right and wrong. Things that the Bible describes as abominations in the sight of the Lord are paraded as alternative lifestyle choices. However, whenever there is true revival, men and women will feel convicted of their sin. They will sense, as never before, the seriousness of living in rebellion against their maker. What John the Baptist calls "the wrath to come" (Matthew 3:7; Luke 3:7) will cease to be a topic of scorn, and will become a pressing reality. People will recognize their danger, and seek the grace of genuine repentance.

The Baptism of the Spirit

In Matthew 3:11 (cf. Mark 1:7–8; Luke 3:16; John 1:33) John the Baptist offers a definition of the work of the one who is coming, for whom he is preparing the way: "he will baptize you with the Holy Spirit." Matthew and Luke add the words "and fire." There is some debate as to the precise meaning of this additional phrase. Some see in the image of fire a reference to judgment, so that the Lord's work is divided into two parts: believers are baptized with the Holy Spirit; unbelievers face the baptism of fire in God's judgment. Alternatively, the fire may be read as an aspect of the baptism of the Holy Spirit.

In support of the first interpretation appeal is made to the immediate context. Both adjacent verses in Matthew, and verses 9 and 17 in Luke, use the metaphor of fire to mean divine judgment, and this is a frequent use of the imagery elsewhere in the New Testament.[4] On the other hand, the second interpretation may be defended on the basis of the grammatical construction. The word "and" links together the Holy Spirit and fire, and the preposition "with" is not repeated before the word "fire." Moreover, the image of fire is sometimes used elsewhere in the New Testament in a positive sense,[5] and it is again used in conjunction with a reference to the Holy Spirit in Acts 2:3 (cf. Revelation 4:5).

I think this second possibility is the more probable meaning here. Just as a fire spreads easily, so the Holy Spirit will apply the work of Christ proclaimed in the gospel in an ever-spreading sphere.

We often tend to think of the baptism of the Holy Spirit in an individual sense. However, that does not seem to be the main way in which the New Testament uses the term. To understand its meaning we need to glance at two passages in the book of Acts.

Shortly before his ascension, Jesus said this to his disciples: "John truly baptized with water, but you shall be baptized with the Holy Spirit not many days from now" (Acts 1:5). Peter refers back to that saying when he tells the church in Jerusalem about the conversion of Cornelius and his household. This is how he puts it in Acts 11:16–17:

> I remembered the word of the Lord, how he said, John indeed baptized with water, but you shall be baptized with the Holy Spirit.'

4. E.g., Matt 5:22; 7:19; 13:40; 18:8–9; 25:41; Mark 9:43, 48; John 15:6; 1 Cor 3:13, 15; 2 Thess 1:8; Heb 10:27; 12:29; 2 Pet 3:7.

5. E.g., Mark 9:49; 1 Pet 1:7.

If therefore God gave them the same gift as he gave us when we believed on the Lord Jesus, who was I that I could withstand God?

These words make it clear that he understood the baptism with the Spirit to have taken place at Pentecost, and that he regarded the events in the house of Cornelius as another baptism with the Spirit in a different place. This points us to the New Testament definition of the baptism with the Spirit. It refers to a special outpouring of the Spirit on a particular place or area, which results in a response to the preaching of God's word in which people are converted in significant numbers. Three thousand people were converted on the day of Pentecost (Acts 2:41), and when the gospel came to the household of Cornelius, "the Holy Spirit fell on all who heard the word" (Acts 10:44). Such outpourings take place as the gospel breaks new ground, but perhaps they may also be expected when the gospel needs to make a fresh impetus in an area where it has stagnated.

Moreover, as is clear from Peter's sermon on the day of Pentecost, the work of the Holy Spirit in such outpourings is to glorify Christ, to extend the sphere of his influence, to secure for him the fulfillment of the Father's promises, to assure to the hearers that Jesus is "both Lord and Christ" (Acts 2:36).

When John the Baptist says to Jesus in Matthew 3:14, "I have need to be baptized by you," he is probably referring back to his statement in verse 11. He is probably not asking Jesus to baptize him in water, but acknowledging that Jesus is the one who must baptize with the Holy Spirit, and that he, John the Baptist, and all his hearers, need to be swept by the Spirit into this fullness of the kingdom, for which his own ministry is merely preparing the way. This remains the crying need of the church at all times.

Jesus' Baptism

As John baptizes Jesus, the Father speaks. He announces to the world that Jesus is his beloved Son. The same words recur on the Mount of Transfiguration (Matthew 17:5; Mark 9:7; Luke 9:35). The Old Testament background to this announcement is found in Genesis 22. Translating the Greek text literally, God calls Jesus "my Son, the beloved" (Matthew 3:17; Mark 1:11; Luke 3:22). In the Septuagint version of Genesis 22 the LORD three times describes Isaac to Abraham as "your son, the beloved" (verses 2, 12, 16). Apart from the changes in person and case, the two phrases are identical.

At the end of Genesis 22 the LORD swears to Abraham like this in verse 18: "in your seed all the nations of the earth shall be blessed." Isaac is the initial seed of Abraham. However, we have noted already that Christ is the true and ultimate seed. As Abraham's initial seed, Isaac points on to him. By echoing his words to Abraham as Jesus is baptized, the Father affirms right at the outset of Jesus' ministry that he is the one in whom the promise of blessing encompassing every nation in the world will be fulfilled. If we can see any nation today which is not enjoying the blessings of the gospel, we have cause to plead the promises in prayer. We have a mandate to pray for a global revival which will make a transforming impact on every single nation.

JESUS' TEMPTATIONS

Matthew and Luke list Jesus' temptations in a different order. Matthew 4:8 and Luke 4:5 describe how the devil takes Jesus to a mountainous vantage point from which he can view "all the kingdoms of the world." He then says: "All these things I will give you if you will fall down and worship me" (Matthew 4:9; cf. Luke 4:6). The devil is suggesting to Jesus an alternative route to achieve the worldwide dominion which he has been promised. Matthew mentions this temptation last. The two earlier temptations had been prefaced by the words, "if you are the Son of God" (Matthew 4:3, 6). The devil is trying to lure Jesus into demonstrating the truth of the Father's announcement at his baptism, but in so doing to divert the privilege he enjoys to his own advantage. That sinister "if you are the Son of God" remains in the background as the final temptation takes place. Luke emphasizes this by placing this temptation in the middle (Luke 4:5–7) between the two "if you are the Son of God" clauses (Luke 4:3, 9). The devil is saying, if Jesus really is God's beloved Son, through whom the blessing of the nations is promised, then let him take the nations and start pouring out his blessing on them. Let him enjoy the prestige of owning the whole world.

In Matthew 4:9 (cf. Luke 4:6) the devil is clearly parodying God's covenant promise to Abraham. He says to Jesus, "all these things I will give you." In Genesis 13:15 the LORD says to Abraham, "all the land which you see I give to you and to your seed forever." This element in the promise is repeated later to Isaac in Genesis 26:3–4: "to you and your seed I give all these lands . . . I will give to your seed all these lands." Now the devil is trying to usurp God's sole right to give the lands of the world to Christ.

But Christ will not fall into this trap. He will await his Father's pleasure. We have the Father's word for it: all the nations on earth will be given to Christ to participate in his blessing. Let us then pray for the fulfillment of these promises in a worldwide outpouring of the Holy Spirit and blessing.

THE GOSPEL OF THE KINGDOM

We read in both Matthew and Mark of the commencement of Jesus' ministry, culminating in his declaration that the kingdom is "at hand" (Matthew 4:12–17; Mark 1:14–15).

The Kingdom at Hand

However, each writer brings out a different truth about the kingdom. Matthew informs us that, to begin with, Jesus centered his ministry around Capernaum, and sees prophetic fulfillment in this. In verses 15–16 he quotes Isaiah 9:1–2. His emphasis is on the endless increase of the kingdom.

The Kingdom's Endless Increase

The striking thing about the Isaiah quotation is the reference to the Gentiles, or the nations. Galilee had a mixed population, with a high proportion of Gentiles. Alec Motyer notes that this began as a result of the failure of the tribes of Zebulun and Naphtali to oust all the Canaanites from the region, and that Solomon's gift of some of the area to Hiram (1 Kings 9:11) contributed further to the growth of a Gentile population here.[6] Another Gentile influx took place with the settlement of the land by the Assyrian invaders. This was followed by further waves of immigration. According to Matthew's quotation of Isaiah's prophecy, these Galilean Gentiles are dwelling in darkness and death, but in the ministry of Jesus the light has dawned upon them.[7] And the thing about dawn is that it implies the full blaze yet to come. The promise here is of ever-increasing light for the Gentile nations, and that light is found in what Jesus calls in verse 17 "the kingdom of heaven."

---

6. Motyer, *Isaiah*, 100.
7. Luke 1:79 also echoes Isa 9:2.

This phrase also links with Isaiah 9. The kingdom of David is mentioned in verse 7. David's kingdom was the representation of heaven's kingdom here on earth. The intervening verses speak of multiplication, joy, liberation and peace, and all because of the birth of the Son who bears the government as he sits on the throne of David's kingdom. Isaiah is clearly looking to Christ. His kingdom will be marked by judgment and justice forever.

But the most relevant thing as far as our present study is concerned is the striking prophecy which Isaiah makes in connection with the birth of the Messiah. He says, "of the increase of his government and of peace there shall be no end." Isaiah prophesies a kingdom in which the government and peace will increase endlessly. He did not merely say that there would be no end to Christ's government, but that there would be no end to his government's increase. It is not just that the kingdom of God as located in Jesus Christ will be endless, but that its increase will be endless.

The gospel has got to keep advancing in this world. The church of Jesus Christ must continuously grow worldwide. More and more nations and tribes and languages and families have obviously got to be drawn into the sphere of gospel blessing. In every place there has to be ongoing gospel expansion. If these things are not so, then the Father has betrayed his promises to his Son, but he cannot do that. If there are times of setback in gospel advance, they can only be temporary, and they must drive us to intercede for the rekindling of gospel fire and the recapture of lost land for Christ.

Jesus' ministry began there in Galilee. The kingdom of heaven came to earth in his work. But that was only the breaking of the dawn. And now his kingdom must go on increasing without interruption throughout the nations of the Gentile world. Christ's kingdom cannot do anything other than grow non-stop. It must happen, because, as Isaiah 9:7 says at the end of the verse, "the zeal of the LORD of hosts will perform this." If ever that growth tails off, if ever decline sets in, if ever in any particular place the growth of Christ's kingdom stops happening, we have an urgent moral duty to cry out to God to intervene in power and to fulfill his word. He waits on our prayers.

The Kingdom's Ultimate Victory

Without using the Isaiah quotation, Mark puts the emphasis on the ultimate victory of what he refers to as "the kingdom of God." This phrase picks up a series of Old Testament texts. Psalm 45 is a Messianic prophecy which emphasizes the righteousness and the eternal duration of God's reign (verse 6). It foresees the LORD's King riding forth majestically and prosperously, until the peoples fall under his sway, prostrating themselves before him in repentance, and gladly submitting to his happy rule (verses 4–5). The Psalm comes to a resounding climax in these words: "I will make your name to be remembered in all generations; therefore the people shall praise you forever and ever" (Psalm 45:17). The Father is promising to secure his Son's victory through the course of the generations of history, until the day arrives when all the world's peoples shall gladly praise his name.

In Daniel 2:44 we hear of a kingdom which God will set up. It is indestructible. It will conquer all other kingdoms, and continue for ever. Daniel refers again to this kingdom in chapter 7. He sees one like the Son of Man receiving an indestructible and eternal kingdom with the purpose and result "that all peoples, nations, and languages should serve him" (verse 13–14). Later in the same chapter we read again, "his kingdom is an everlasting kingdom, and all dominions shall serve and obey him" (verse 27).

This is the kingdom of God which is "at hand" in the ministry of Jesus, who so often referred to himself as "the Son of Man." He has brought the kingdom down into this world, and we now anticipate the fulfillment of the prophecies concerning that kingdom—its uninterrupted expansion, its victory in every people group on earth. These are the promises which should shape our faith and fuel our prayers.

The Kingdom our First Priority

Jesus teaches us to pray, "your kingdom come" (Matthew 6:10; Luke 11:2), and it is the fulfillment of the prophecies which will constitute the answer to this prayer. If people are not being converted in ever growing numbers everywhere, then that has to be our dominant burden in prayer. "Your kingdom come" really is the prayer for worldwide revival, and Jesus makes it the very first petition in his model prayer after the opening expression of worship. Prayer for revival should always be our first priority.

Jesus' words in Matthew 6:33 (cf. Luke 12:31) also emphasize the primacy of this concern: "Seek first the kingdom of God and his righteousness." Jesus makes this exhortation at the end of a passage in which he has been urging his disciples not to succumb to anxiety. He notes that the unbelieving Gentile nations seek the things they need for life in this world—especially food and clothing (Matthew 6:32; Luke 12:30), and urges us not to be like them: "do not seek what you should eat or what you should drink" (Luke 12:29). The word "seek" can speak of an all-consuming craving, of the pursuit of the things which are our main ambition in life. For the unbeliever, survival and comfort, pleasure and display, are the major preoccupations. The Christian, however, has higher goals. Our overriding desire, our burning passion is to see the kingdom of God in Christ triumph in this world. That is what we seek constantly in our prayers and by our efforts for the gospel. Jesus assures us that, if God's interests in the world are our priority interest, then God will look after us in worldly matters.

The Destiny of the Kingdom

That the kingdom of God, as it has come in Jesus Christ, will triumph in the world is the message of some of the parables of the kingdom. The parable of the mustard seed (Matthew 13:31–32; Mark 8:30–32; Luke 13:18–19) tells how, from the tiniest of seeds, a great tree will grow. The birth of a baby in Bethlehem and the death of a man on a cross may seem trivial and insignificant. And yet this is the origin of the kingdom. This is the seed out of which a worldwide spiritual empire emerges. The parable of the leaven (Matthew 13:33; Luke 13:20–21) describes the all-pervading influence of that kingdom, which is destined truly and totally to transform all human societies. These parables are designed to excite our anticipation and to stimulate our prayers.

The Kingdom Present with Power

On one occasion Jesus said that some of his immediate hearers would live "to see the Son of Man coming in his kingdom" (Matthew 16:28). Mark's rendering is, "there are some standing here who will not taste death till they see the kingdom of God present with power" (Mark 9:1; cf. Luke 9:27). Clearly no one has yet seen the second coming of Jesus, and no one has yet seen the global triumph of the gospel in every nation simultaneously. So Jesus cannot have been referring to either of these two future events. So what did he mean by these words?

The most likely explanation is that he was speaking of his own resurrection and ascension, and of the outpouring of the Spirit at Pentecost. In the Old Testament, the kingdom was anticipated. In the life of Christ, the kingdom was at hand. Because of his resurrection and then his exaltation at the Father's right hand the Spirit has been outpoured, and so the kingdom is now present with power. All that we wait for is the exertion of that power into all the world, so that the day of universal gospel glory shall come, and then Christ will return to deliver the kingdom to his Father (1 Corinthians 15:24). That is the vision which must drive us to pray for its full realization.

The Sign of the End

Jesus taught that the fulfillment of this gospel advance and the establishment of his reign through the gospel worldwide would be the only sign of his return. The disciples once drew Jesus' attention to the splendor of the temple. They were commenting on "how it was adorned with beautiful stones" (Luke 21:5). Mark quotes their exact words: "Teacher, see what manner of stones and what buildings are here!" (Mark 13:1). For the Jews the temple was the supreme symbol of their national excellence. Jesus immediately drops a bombshell: "Do you see these great buildings? Not one stone shall be left upon another, that shall not be thrown down." (Mark 13:2; cf. Matthew 24:2; Luke 21:6). This prompts the disciples, as soon as the opportunity arises, to ask Jesus a question: "Tell us, when will these things be? And what will be the sign of your coming, and of the end of the age?" (Matthew 24:3). Jesus had not actually said anything about the end of the age, but to a devout Jew the temple was so sacred, that he could not imagine that its destruction could mean anything but the end of the world.

Jesus now has to clarify the situation and overcome their confusion. He separates two things that must be kept apart—the end, which he speaks about in Matthew 24:4-14 (cf. Mark 13:5-13; Luke 21:8-19), and the destruction of Jerusalem, which is his theme in verses 15-26 (cf. Mark 13:14-23; Luke 21:20-24), before he resumes talking about the last days.

It is sometimes said that Jesus gives us a number of signs of the nearness of the end in Matthew 24:6-12. Jesus mentions wars, famines, epidemics, earthquakes, persecution, error, and lawlessness. However, it is wrong to read these as signs of the end. Jesus says emphatically in verse 6, "the end is not yet." In verse 8 he describes these phenomena not as the end, but "the beginning of sorrows." Such things are not signs of the end, but challenges to keep on enduring until the end comes (verse 13). The fact is, these things are permanent features of a fallen world; they have been happening for centuries.

Actually, Jesus names only one sign of the end, and we find it in verse 14: "this gospel of the kingdom will be preached in all the world as a witness to all the nations, and then the end will come." We can start to think that the end might be near only when the gospel has been proclaimed worldwide, and has been powerfully effective in every single nation on earth, with no nation bypassed or left untouched.

That I take to be the significance of the word "witness." It is a word which Jesus uses again in Luke 24:48 and in Acts 1:8, where he commissions the apostles as witnesses. "Witness" is a term borrowed from the law courts. But a witness does not just talk for the sake of it in a kind of "take-it-or-leave-it" fashion. A witness speaks passionately about what he has seen and knows, and his testimony is designed to secure a conviction. By using this word, Jesus seems to imply not that the gospel will be preached everywhere but most people will simply ignore it, but that the passionate preaching of the gospel by people who know that it is the truth will in fact secure conviction worldwide. The nations as a whole will be convinced that Jesus is the Lord of all and will bow to his supremacy. That ought to be our sincere expectation, and this expectation ought to be driving us constantly to prayer for worldwide revival.

There are two things about Jesus' words in verse 14 which are noteworthy. The first is that he uses a different word for "end" than the one used by the disciples in verse 3. They were thinking about the termination of everything. He redirects their attention to the ultimate climax of everything. Imagine a conversation about a one-day limited over cricket match. Bill asks Ben, "When will this end?" He's wondering whether he'll be able to go home on the 6 o'clock bus, or whether he'll have to wait until 6.30. Ben replies, "I can't wait to see the end." By "the end" Ben means the last two or three overs when everything reaches an exciting climax. The team batting second will be involved in a ferocious run chase, while the bowling side will be striving as hard as possible to take the last two wickets.

When Jesus speaks of "the end" it's more like Ben's use of the term. For Jesus "the end" is the climax, the final period of history when everything accelerates to its exciting fulfillment, when all that God has been working towards down through the millennia finally becomes reality. "The end" is not just a full-stop. It's the glorious goal. It's not just a moment of time. It's a period of gospel blessing transforming the whole world. It will happen when Jesus clearly reigns as king over all the nations.

The second thing about Jesus' words is that he uses a less common word for "come." It really means not simply "to come," but "to have come." So verse 14 means that the gospel will be preached to all nations in its effective convicting power, and then the climax will have come. We look forward to that climax. We must therefore pray for the Holy Spirit's power to be poured out upon the preaching of the gospel, so that through the gospel every nation is transformed, and the climax of God's purposes is achieved throughout the world. A Bible-believing Christian can never be a pessimist. In faith, we expect to see God's word fulfilled. We believe that revival will break out simultaneously everywhere.

The Kingdom "Not of This World"

Jesus' trial revolved around the question whether or not he was a king.[8] John cites Jesus' answer to Pilate's question whether he is a king:

> My kingdom is not of this world. If my kingdom were of this world, my servants would fight, so that I should not be delivered to the Jews; but now my kingdom is not from here (John 18:36).

What we have said about the historical fulfillment of the prophecies of the coming of the kingdom, might seem to be at odds with Jesus' statement that his kingdom is not of this world. However, Jesus is not saying that his kingdom will never achieve historical realization within the present world. He is talking about the source of his kingdom, which is heavenly, and the means of its progress, which does not use worldly methods.

The Kingdom Filled

Luke 14:16–24 recounts the parable of the great supper. It is precipitated by a comment made by "one of those who sat at the table with him." He said: "Blessed is he who shall eat bread in the kingdom of God" (verse 15). The parable is directed against those who presumptuously assumed that they were automatically enrolled in the kingdom. When the summons to attend the supper was issued, "they all with one accord began to make excuses." The master then sent his servant first "into the streets and lanes of the city," to gather as many people as he could find, regardless of whether they were

---

8. See Matt 27:11, 29, 37, 42; Mark 15:2, 9, 12, 18, 26, 32; Luke 23:2–3, 37–38; John 18:33, 36–37, 39; 19:3, 12, 14–15, 19, 21.

poor, maimed, lame or blind. Once this order had been obeyed the servant had to report to his master, "still there is room." The master therefore sent the servant out in to the countryside. The essential thing was that the house must "be filled." The message of the parable is that God's kingdom will be filled with unlikely people gathered together from everywhere. Jesus is looking forward to the ingathering of the Gentile nations. Our responsibility in evangelism and in prayer is to gather the urban and rural outcasts from every nation, until the whole earth resembles that kingdom supper.

JESUS AND THE CROWDS

In the course of Jesus' ministry he was often surrounded by great crowds. As early as Matthew 4:24–25 we hear of his fame spreading, and huge crowds of people coming from all over the place to follow him.

Multitudes

References to the "great multitudes" who thronged around him are repeated numerous times in the Gospels.[9] One particularly striking comment is found in Luke 12:1: "an innumerable multitude of people had gathered together, so that they trampled one another." Mark tells of an occasion when a "whole city was gathered together" to listen to Jesus (Mark 1:33). The next day Simon Peter could say to Jesus, "Everyone is looking for you" (Mark 1:37).

This is the first instalment of the progress of Jesus' kingdom. The crowds that flocked to hear him are the precursors of those countless souls from every nation who, in the course of history, will meet Jesus in the preaching of the gospel and follow him. Jesus seems to indicate this in Matthew 8:11. The chapter has begun by noting that "great multitudes followed him." Then a Roman centurion steps out of the crowd and pleads with Jesus to heal his servant. The conversation that ensues reveals the centurion's "great faith"—a faith so remarkable that even Jesus marveled (verse 10). Jesus' response to this declaration of faith by a Gentile is to say, "many will come from east and west and sit down with Abraham, Isaac, and Jacob

---

9. Matt 8:1, 18; 12:15; 13:2; 14:14; 15:30, 33; 19:2; 20:29; 21:8; Mark 3:7–8; 4:1; 5:21, 24; 6:34; 8:1; 10:46; Luke 5:15; 6:17; 8:4; 9:37; 14:25; 23:27; John 6:2, 5.

in the kingdom of heaven." Jesus more or less repeats this statement in a different context in Luke 13:28–29.

Many

The word "many" is another one which recurs frequently in the Gospels, to describe the large numbers of people who wanted to listen to Christ. It is interesting how often it is used to emphasize that many most unlikely people followed Christ—those who were demon possessed,[10] tax-collectors and sinners,[11] the sick,[12] foreigners.[13] The parable of the wedding feast also makes the point that many unlikely candidates will be admitted into Christ's kingdom (Matthew 22:9–10). So it is in the statement of Matthew 8:11. Many people will come from all directions, from all nations, from outside the chosen people of Israel, to be part of the kingdom which Jesus has brought to earth. That is a certainty. That is our confidence.

All the references in the Gospels to "the many" are gathered up in the statements which tell us that Jesus came "to give his life a ransom for many" (Matthew 20:28; Mark 10:45), and that his blood "was shed for many for the remission of sins" (Matthew 26:28; cf. Mark 14:24). The many are the people from every nation under heaven for whom he shed his blood and gave his life, so that they could become part of his kingdom. The choice of this word "many" stresses the point that God's elect must never be seen as "a chosen few." To interpret Jesus' two statements that "few are chosen" (Matthew 20:16; 22:14) to mean that few people will believe in any generation is to wrest them right out of context. God's elect are "a great multitude which no one could number, of all nations, tribes, peoples and tongues" (Revelation 7:9). The whole thrust of the Bible's story line is towards ever-widening universalism. As the centuries roll by more and more of God's elect, in inevitably increasing numbers, must be gathered into Christ's kingdom, until that day when this kingdom has the supremacy in every nation on earth. We must therefore pray for the kingdom to come, and the many to be brought to faith in the Savior.

---

10. Matt 8:16; Mark 1:34; Luke 4:41; 7:21.

11. Matt 9:10; Mark 2:15.

12. Matt 14:36; 15:30; Mark 1:34; 3:10; 6:13, 56; Luke 7:21.

13. John 4:39, 41.

A Bumper Harvest

But for this to happen, laborers are needed. So Jesus urges us to "pray the Lord of the harvest to send out laborers into his harvest" (Matthew 9:38). He has just said that "the harvest truly is plentiful, but the laborers are few" (verse 37). He said something very similar to his disciples following his conversation with the Samaritan woman:

> Do you not say, "There are four months and then comes the har-
> vest"? Behold, I say to you, lift up your eyes and look at the fields,
> for they are already white for harvest (John 4:35).

When Jesus speaks of four months until harvest, he is speaking of the literal agricultural situation of that season of the year. However, the second part of his comment refers to the spiritual harvest, the waiting harvest of souls for his kingdom. Jesus is telling us that we must never delay our efforts to reap a harvest of souls on the pretext that we are not living in a reaping season. There is always a bumper harvest just waiting to be gathered in.

In the pessimistic spirit that prevails today we tend to think that Jesus was wrong when he made these statements. It's not true that there is a plentiful harvest, we protest. We are living in a season of sowing. All that confronts us as we proclaim the gospel of Christ is apathy and hostility. We live in barren times. This is the day of small things. We may sow the seed, but we have lost the expectancy that we shall do anything much in the way of reaping a harvest. Once again, we have become closet theological liberals. We explain away what Jesus said in the light of the circumstances which we know, rather than seeking to interpret the circumstances in the light of the word of Christ. There is a massive harvest just waiting to be gathered in. We know there is, because Jesus says so. And to make sure that we get the message, he adds the word "truly" in Matthew 9:37. This is true. To deny it is to accuse Jesus Christ of being a liar.

In John 4:38 Jesus says, "I have sent you to reap." But, we might retort, Jesus was only talking about his day and age. He didn't experience the apostasy and error that prevails in contemporary western culture. So what he said then, doesn't apply now. But look at his impression of the people of his own generation. They are described in Matthew 9:36 as weary, scattered, and shepherdless. The word "weary" means exhausted and despondent. The word "scattered" means facing pressures that bring you to the very edge of being unable to cope. Whenever people do not know the Good Shepherd they really are shepherdless, because there is no other valid shepherd to guide them safely through life. Are these terms not just as accurate a description of people now as then? Well, that is precisely the situation which makes Jesus conclude that there is a bumper harvest just waiting to be gathered in. If ever we think that the scene looks ripe for judgment, we have to remember that that also means that it is ripe for mercy, and that "mercy triumphs over judgment" (James 2:13). All we need is laborers who will preach the message of hope. And we are commanded to pray that the Lord would raise up preachers of the gospel so that this waiting harvest can be immediately reaped. Here is an explicit New Testament command to pray for revival.

JESUS' MIRACLES

In Matthew 8:16, we read of "many who were demon-possessed" who came to Jesus. Jesus "cast out the spirits with a word, and healed all who were sick." Matthew goes on, in verses 17–18, to cite this as the fulfillment of Isaiah 53:4: "He himself took our infirmities, and bore our sicknesses."

"Healing Revival"?

Occasionally we hear the suggestion that healing is part of revival. The term "healing revival" was used of a movement associated with William Branham, Oral Roberts, and others, which lasted from 1947 to 1958.[14] More recently it was used in connection with the now discredited work of Todd Bentley in Florida around 2008.[15] Now, I certainly do not wish to deny that God may heal miraculously when he so chooses. However, to read Isaiah in the light of Matthew makes it clear that healing is not revival, and that we are not to chase miracles of healing as we pray for revival.

The effect of Matthew's quotation is to set Jesus' miracles in the context of his atoning death, and to emphasize the subservient place which his miracles hold in relation to his main work of offering satisfaction for sin. Isaiah 53:4 begins with the words which Matthew says were fulfilled in Jesus' healing ministry. It then continues, "yet we esteemed him stricken, smitten by God, and afflicted." The word "esteemed" has the sense of

14. Harrell, *All Things are Possible*, 23–132.
15. See Strom, *Todd Bentley*.

making a judgment about something.[16] Isaiah's prophecy is saying that we see how Jesus healed so many sick people, and yet, in spite of his gracious work of healing, it was Jesus' suffering which dominated people's estimate of him. When it comes to making a judgment about the heart of his work, it is not his healings which we focus on; that is not where the essence of his ministry is found. His healings are somewhat incidental to his mission. They are certainly not the central phenomenon. Rather, it is the sufferings of Christ which claim our attention when we seek to define who he was and why he came. The following verses go on to explain the substitutionary and penal nature of those sufferings, and then Isaiah looks beyond the suffering to the glory, as he speaks of the amazing fruit of Christ's sufferings.

Verse 10 speaks of prolonged days in which the LORD's will prospers in the hand of Christ. Verse 11 speaks of Christ's satisfaction as the many are justified as a result of his work. Verse 12 says that he will receive the spoils of his victory, and directly links the victory to the penal substitutionary suffering as its cause. Verse 12 includes the words "he was numbered with the transgressors." Twice in the gospels these words are quoted as fulfilled at Calvary (Mark 15:28; Luke 22:37).

Isaiah 53 leads on into chapter 54. The first three verses of that chapter celebrate Christ's numerous spiritual offspring, the constant enlargement and expansion of his kingdom, and his inheritance of the nations. That is revival. So the context in Isaiah of Matthew's quotation warns us not to get hung up on healing. That is not the meaning of revival. Revival is the conversion of expanding numbers of sinners who are justified by Christ's death, their sins forgiven, and their lives transformed into the energetic pursuit of holiness.

John the Baptist's Messengers

In Matthew 11:2–3 we read of the messengers whom John the Baptist sent to Jesus. John is in prison, and is wondering whether he was mistaken to see Jesus as "the Coming One." His question now is, "do we look for another?" In reply to the messengers Jesus refers to his miracles. Verse 5 reads as follows:

---

16. *Theological Wordbook of the Old Testament*, #767.

the blind see and the lame walk; the lepers are cleansed and the deaf hear; the dead are raised up and the poor have the gospel preached to them.

The wording here intentionally recalls the prophecies of Isaiah. As a result, the miracles are portrayed as signs that Jesus is the one in whom the prophetic promises are fulfilled.

It seems that there are four main passages from Isaiah in Jesus' mind as he speaks these words. We shall look at them each in turn.

Isaiah 29:18

This verse reads like this:

> In that day the deaf shall hear the words of the book, and the eyes of the blind shall see out of obscurity and out of darkness.

This lies behind Jesus' statements that "the blind see" and "the deaf hear." But Isaiah's words show that Jesus does not enable deaf people to hear again just for the sake of it. It is specifically so that they may "hear the words of the book." Physical deafness is symbolic. It reflects the deeper deafness which afflicts all human beings in our sinful nature—we are deaf to the word of God, unable to make sense of divine truth. Earlier in chapter 29 Isaiah has spoken of the sealing of the book (verses 11–12). It is an act of divine judgment to remove the wisdom and insight which only his truth can confer. Jesus' healing miracles symbolize the real purpose of his mission: to restore spiritually deaf sinners to the hearing and understanding of the truth. The first phrase of Isaiah's text throws light on the second. The blindness in view is also primarily spiritual. The obscurity and darkness are the confusion and ignorance which result when sin has engulfed the world. It is the same darkness referred to in Isaiah 9:2, and the blindness is the same as that already mentioned in Isaiah 29—in verses 9–10: the blindness that results when the LORD pours out the spirit of deep sleep upon a sinful people and closes their eyes to his word. When Jesus restored sight to blind men, it was a signal that the true reason for his coming was to fulfill the prophecies of an end to the moral obscurity and spiritual night that has descended upon the entire human family.

But Isaiah sets this prophecy in the context of "that day." This phrase which opens verse 18 refers back to the previous verse, which speaks of a day when "Lebanon shall be turned into a fruitful field, and the fruitful field be esteemed as a forest." This verse links with Isaiah 32:15, which anticipates the day when the Spirit will be poured out from on high. On that day "the wilderness becomes a fruitful field, and the fruitful field is counted as a forest." The following verses depict the social life of that time. It will be marked by justice, righteousness, peace, security, and blessing. The opening verse of the chapter says, "Behold, a king will reign in righteousness." That sets the scene for the rest of the passage. It is when Jesus Christ, the righteous king, reigns on earth that the era of peace and justice will be established. This is achieved through the outpouring of the Holy Spirit. We must therefore pray that the Father will fulfill his word, pour out the Spirit in every place, and bring to earth's nations and peoples the justice and peace which they crave, but which must remain ever elusive until Jesus' reign is established worldwide. We must pray for that global revival.

Isaiah 35:5–6

Here is the second passage to which Jesus' words allude:

> Then the eyes of the blind shall be opened, and the ears of the deaf shall be unstopped; then the lame shall leap like a deer, and the tongue of the dumb shall sing.

Here again we have mention of the blind and the deaf. Isaiah also mentions the lame, another theme which Jesus picks up in his words to John the Baptist's messengers. Isaiah's previous verse tells us that these miracles of healing will take place when God comes to save his people, and from the second half of verse 6 we have the explanation of why these things will happen at that time. It is because the waters will flow, reviving the land. We may compare these words with Isaiah 44:3: "I will pour water on him who is thirsty, and floods on the dry ground; I will pour my Spirit on your descendants, and my blessing on your offspring." For Isaiah, waters represent the Holy Spirit. It is when his life flows into the world that this transformation will take place. Well, in Jesus, God has come to save, the Spirit is outpoured, and spiritually stultified lives are renewed.

The rest of Isaiah 35 depicts the LORD's redeemed returning to Zion. Their journey will be direct, safe, and marked by abundant happiness. But, perhaps most significantly, they will walk "the Highway of Holiness," and there will be no place on that road for the unclean (verse 8). When the Holy

Spirit comes in true revival, the fruit of holiness will always be evident in the lives of Christ's people.

One of the tragedies of a situation like our present one, where the power of the gospel is not very apparent, where the church is in decline and the culture careers ever deeper into the moral abyss, is that professing Christians become careless and morally lax. They become terribly infected by the blatantly sinful environment that surrounds us. A young woman claims to be a Christian, and yet shamelessly lives with a "partner." A young man professes faith, and yet brazenly continues to sleep with his girlfriends. An older man says that he is a Christian, and yet he is cynically dishonest in his business dealings or in legal matters. An older woman pretends to be a believer, and yet thinks nothing of being permanently grumpy, critical, and arrogant. The spirit of the age creeps into the church, and the believer's way of life becomes indistinguishable from that of the world. When there is revival, all that inevitably changes. Holiness becomes a gripping reality in the hearts of God's people. Morally lax professing evangelical Christians are startled to find that they were never truly converted at all. They either repent and come to Christ, or they disappear from the scene, terrified to continue having any involvement with the things of God. In praying for revival, one of the imperatives is that we must pray for the restoration of holiness.

In these first two passages from Isaiah's prophecy, there has been no explicit reference to the world as a whole. The initial concern is the people of Israel. We might well therefore hesitate to apply them more widely, and ask whether we are justified in so doing. This changes when we come to the third of our four passages, and in the light of how Isaiah now continues, it seems legitimate to read back into the earlier passages hope not just for Israel, but for all the nations of the world.

Isaiah 42

In his words to John the Baptist's messengers, Jesus refers, as we have already noted, to the blind and the deaf. Both categories are mentioned again in this chapter. The blind figure in verses 7, 16, 18 and 19, and the deaf also in verses 18–19.

In verses 6–7 the LORD is directly addressing his servant. However, before we turn our attention to the content of those verses, we need to turn back to Matthew's Gospel. Matthew 12:17–21 indicates that the servant prophecies are ultimately fulfilled in Jesus Christ. Jesus has just healed great crowds of people, and then urged them not to make him known. In this Matthew sees a fulfillment of Isaiah 42:1–4, which he quotes in full. This passage looks forward to the proclamation of justice to all nations, and to the steady progress of the gospel until justice is victoriously established, and the Gentiles find their hope in Christ. Moreover, the quotation makes it clear that this will happen because of the presence of the Spirit. By using this quotation, Matthew yet again brings Old Testament prophetic promises within the scope of a genuine New Testament theology of revival. We are challenged to pray that God will fulfill his promises to Christ, that all the nations of the Gentile world will acknowledge Christ as their only hope, that justice may thrive on earth.

The references to the blind and the deaf in Isaiah 42 follow on from those introductory verses which open the chapter. In verses 6–7 the LORD tells Christ that he is given to the Gentile peoples, "to open blind eyes, to bring out prisoners from the prison, those who sit in darkness from the prison house." Clearly, the blind here are the Gentiles. It is a description which Paul also uses for the Gentile world in Romans 2:19, and he accounts for the blindness of the Gentiles like this: "they do not have the law by nature"[17] (Romans 2:14). God's law was not part of their cultural background. Possession of the law was a privilege which was not accorded to the Gentiles. Consequently, they grew up in moral and spiritual ignorance. They were in the dark. They were blind. But Christ's mission changes all that. The Gentile nations are brought out of the captivity of darkness into the glorious light of the gospel.

However, it is not only the Gentiles who are blind. In Isaiah 42:16–18 it is Israel, the initial, partial, inadequate servant of the LORD, who is blind. But now the true servant, Jesus Christ, promises to "make darkness light before them" (verse 16), and appeals to his own people, "look, you blind, that you may see" (verse 18). Likewise, the deaf, mentioned in verses 18–19, are the LORD's messenger, the people of Israel, and Christ cries out to them, "Hear, you deaf." Now we realize that spiritual and moral blindness and deafness afflict the entire human race, Jew and Gentile alike. But here we also catch a glimpse of the ultimate biblical vision of the entire world, Jew and Gentile, Israel and all the nations, reunited with spiritual vision and hearing as the single human family in Christ, the true representative of the human race. But for that to happen the gospel must be preached effectively

17. For a defense of this way of punctuating the text, see Bayes, *Weakness*, 104–7.

in every part of the world. As long as there is one Gentile nation which is not yet transformed by the power of the gospel, as long as the Jews remain in ignorance of the fact that Jesus is the Messiah, then we must pray urgently, fervently, constantly, for the outpouring of the Spirit, for the raising up of laborers for the harvest field, for the empowering of the preaching of the gospel, until we see the day of glory dawn on earth. We dare not relegate these promises to the mists of eternity. To do so is to empty the Scriptures of much of their relevance to life in the present age. It is to rest content with a personal salvation, but to fail to share the Father's concern for the reputation of his Son. If Jesus is not clearly recognized as Lord of all worldwide, then we have much praying still to do, until the Spirit comes and drives home the victory which has been guaranteed to Jesus by the prophecies of God's word.

Isaiah 61:1

Here is the final passage which lies behind Jesus' words to John the Baptist's messengers:

> The Spirit of the Lord GOD is upon me, because the Lord has anointed me to preach good tidings to the poor.

One piece of Jesus' evidence for John the Baptist that he was "the coming one" was that "the poor have the gospel preached to them." Those words are a direct allusion to this text from Isaiah. Jesus referred to Isaiah 61 even more explicitly at the synagogue in Nazareth. He read verses 1–2, and then affirmed that he himself was the one anointed with the Spirit of the LORD, as he said, "Today this Scripture is fulfilled in your hearing" (Luke 4:16–21).

In Isaiah 61 the word "poor" forms a sort of heading. The chapter goes on to speak of the broken-hearted, the captives, those who are bound, those who mourn, and of people living in a situation of ruin and desolation. The equivalent list in Luke's Gospel is the broken-hearted, the captives, the blind, and the oppressed. The word "poor" sums up all those conditions. To these poor people, in these various categories of poverty, Jesus preaches the good news of the gospel. This is a poverty which is not necessarily material and financial. It afflicts the heart, the spirit. When people are held captive by their sins, they are the poor who are bound.

This is clear from the way the passage is translated in Luke's Gospel. Luke is following the Septuagint here. The reference to the blind replaces the mention of those who are bound. Luke's next reference to the blind comes in chapter 6:39. It means those who cannot see the right way through life. It is those who are bound in the darkness of sin and unbelief by moral blindness that Isaiah is concerned about. The oppressed is an additional category, not found in the Isaiah passage. The word used occurs only here in the New Testament, though it occurs several times in the Septuagint. Its most significant use for our purposes is found in Isaiah 58:6, where it occurs in parallel with terms associated with bondage and heavy burdens. Moreover, it is notable that the word almost always occurs in a context which speaks of God's judgment.[18] It emphasizes that we are speaking of people oppressed by the conditions of a sinful world, a world permanently marked by the signs of God's judgment.

Isaiah 61 goes on to portray the transformation in the circumstances of these morally and spiritually poor people that results when the gospel is proclaimed to them. Ruins are rebuilt, desolate cities are repaired. Gentiles are serving Israel, while Israel is serving God. The world's wealth and resources are pooled to the glory of God. Shame is replaced by honor, and confusion by joy. The LORD personally directs his people's work in truth, and blessing rests upon them. And all this is founded on the truth and the joyful experience of justification in Christ, which the LORD God will cause "to spring forth before all the nations" (verse 11). At Nazareth, by his references to the Sidonian widow at Zarephath and to Naaman (Luke 4:26–27), Jesus has already implied that his goal is the conversion of the nations. The verb "spring forth" in Isaiah 61:11 speaks of the growth of a plant or of hair. It speaks of continuous growth. It speaks of growth that cannot be halted. It speaks of abundant growth. So we live in the age when spiritually impoverished souls have the gospel preached to them, enter into justification in Christ, and become part of a worldwide, trans-national company of people, that grows incessantly through every generation. If where we are we cannot see uninterrupted growth, then we are under obligation to cry out to the Lord to reverse the decline, and to fulfill his word.

THE CHURCH AND THE GATES OF HELL

In Matthew 16:18 Jesus says to his disciples, "I will build my church, and the gates of Hades shall not prevail against it." Peter has just acted as spokesman

---

18. See Exod 15:6; Num 16:46; 24:17; Deut 28:33; 2 Sam 12:15; 2 Chr 6:24; 20:37; Job 20:19; Isa 2:10, 19, 21; Jer 51:30; Ezek 21:7, 15.

for the disciples. Jesus has asked them who they say that he is. Verse 16 tells us, "Simon Peter answered and said, 'You are the Christ, the Son of the living God.'" Jesus then stresses the significance of the name Peter, which means "rock," and says, "on this rock I will build my church."

On the Rock

There has been much discussion as to what Jesus meant by "this rock." Various answers have been given, and it is probably not necessary to choose one to the exclusion of all the others. Jesus may have meant that the rock was Peter as the representative of the apostles, who together formed the first generation foundation of the church through their church planting ministry, and their role as the inspired witnesses who gave us the New Testament (Ephesians 2:20).

Or he may have meant that he himself was "this rock." Certainly, he is the ultimate foundation of the church, whatever subsidiary foundational role the apostles might fulfill (1 Corinthians 3:11).

Again, Jesus could have been referring to Peter's confession. That Jesus is "the Christ, the Son of the living God," is the foundational truth on which the church must stand, or else it falls to ruin. Jesus had to go on just a few verses later to emphasize some of the implications of describing him like this, which the disciples might otherwise have overlooked:

> From that time Jesus began to show to his disciples that he must go to Jerusalem, and suffer many things from the elders and chief priests and scribes, and be killed, and be raised the third day (verse 21).

To confess Jesus as the Christ, the Son of God, includes confessing his atoning sufferings, his sacrificial death, and his resurrection to glory and power.

Whichever shades of meaning are included in Jesus' words, what follows is clear. On the foundation of Christ, the apostles, and the sound confession of truth, Jesus will build his church and hell's gates will not be able to prevail against it.

Although the exact word which Jesus used was "Hades," I think it is legitimate to render it as "hell." Hendriksen notes "how sharply it is contrasted with 'heaven,'" and points to Luke 16:23–24, where Hades is the place of torment. He concludes, "probably everywhere in the *Gospels*, but not everywhere in the entire New Testament, Hades means 'hell.'"[19]

In the past, when I read Matthew 16:18, I use to picture a cringing little church, assailed by the powerful gates of hell, which towered massively over the tiny church. And yet somehow, by the skin of its teeth, the church was just about managing to hold on in there, and avoid total annihilation. Then it occurred to me: armies don't usually carry the gates of their city or their barracks with them when they advance into battle. They generally leave the gates behind! The gates are not hell's weapons of attack, with which to try to beat the puny, struggling church into oblivion. The picture is the total opposite of that one.

On the Advance

It is the church that is on the advance. It is hell which is cringing. Hell is cowering with terror as Christ's church strides across the earth. Hell's gates are securely closed. They are her last line of defense against the victorious church. Everywhere the church goes, the battering ram of the gospel hammers against the gates of hell. Everywhere the gospel penetrates, hell's gates crack and shudder and shatter, and souls once held in sin's deadly grip are led through the gates to joyful safety in Christ.

Dick France shows rather a lack of imagination when he rejects the possibility that this text supports "the picturesque idea of an attack on death's gates by the church." He dismisses this interpretation of the verse with a rather scornful question: "What could this mean? A sort of *descensus ad inferos* by the church?!"[20] France's exclamation mark seems to be the written equivalent of "ha ha ha." Such a comment suggests that he fails to understand the inextricable link between sin, Satan, death, and hell, which makes it possible for Jesus to refer to hell as a summary term embracing all the others. As Jesus' church advances, Satan hides behind his gates. But he knows for sure that his time is up, that the nations of the world, enslaved by sin and death, shall be liberated to serve the living God, that Christ's kingdom will triumph, that the kingdom of evil shall be ousted from its supremacy, that his days as "the god of this age" (2 Corinthians 4:4) are numbered, that he is well and truly defeated.

19. Hendriksen, *Matthew*, 496.
20. France, *Matthew*, 255–56.

I admit that this reading of Matthew 16:18 is not widespread. However, I am glad to discover that I am not totally alone in understanding it like this. The late Bob Passantino and his wife Gretchen were American Lutheran evangelical Christians who headed up an organisation called *Answers in Action*. Its main work was in the field of Apologetics, particularly towards the victims of the cults. In an article entitled *The Gates of Hell*, they point out that the Lord here gives us "a bold promise." They agree that a gate is a defensive weapon, and comment: "A gate keeps attackers out of one's fortress. So, if the gates of Hades or hell cannot prevail against the church, that must mean that the church will mount a successful offense against the powers of evil . . . In other words, when the gates 'will not prevail,' that means that the church, in effect, knocks down the gates." The Passantinos then go on to say that one sense in which this is true is in "the promulgation of the gospel in the world, converting men from the kingdom of the devil to the kingdom of God."

In support of this interpretation of our verse, the Passantinos refer to the story told in Acts which documents the rapid spread of the gospel and growth of the church during its first few decades. They then cite 2 Corinthians 10:3–5:

> we do not war according to the flesh. For the weapons of our warfare are not carnal but mighty in God for pulling down strongholds, casting down arguments and every high thing that exalts itself against the knowledge of God, bringing every thought into captivity to the obedience of Christ.[21]

This verse certainly portrays an advancing church demolishing hell's fortifications, and leading sinners out of hell's captivity into the glorious liberty of obedience to Christ.

I like Paul's phrase "not carnal but mighty." I think if we had written it, we might have said "not carnal but nevertheless mighty." The church doesn't fight with guns and bombs, but somehow, in spite of that, we seem to get by. That seems at least to be the general mentality amongst Christians in this country today. That's why we have capitulated to fear of jihadist Islam. They seem to have all the might, because their weapons are carnal. We don't have carnal weapons, but, against all the odds, God gives our spiritual weapons some power, so that we just about survive. Paul's words are very different. We could paraphrase them, "the weapons of our warfare are not

---

21. Passantino & Passantino, *Gates of Hell*, lines 26–34, 47–49.

carnal so therefore they are mighty." Of course they are. We do not wage the good fight with mere carnal weapons like guns and bombs. What hope would there be for us if we did? God has given us something far more powerful than those ultimately useless things. He has given us the gospel. It has changed our lives. It has made us men and women of love. It is leading sinners worldwide to Jesus. It is transforming nations. It is ensuring the dawn of an era of peace and justice.

The Passantinos' article concludes that, in the light of Matthew 16:18, "we can go confidently into the world with the message of the gospel, knowing that the power of the resurrected Christ goes with us—and that there is no one who is so trapped by the power of the devil that the power of the gospel cannot reach that person with God's grace and mercy. To the contrary, everywhere the gospel is preached the church triumphs over evil, the kingdom expands and evil retreats."[22]

In verse 19, indeed, Jesus connects his church with the kingdom of heaven. The church is the kingdom's key holder. Luke 11:52 refers to "the key of knowledge." The key is the gospel, the message which brings to a sinful world the knowledge of God's wonderful provision in Christ for their salvation. As the advancing church proclaims the gospel, the kingdom is unlocked and countless men and women from every nation pour in through the open door of invitation and welcome and mercy. And so the kingdom of Christ on earth expands and grows exponentially. That is the prospect which the New Testament holds out to us. Is the church growing at that rate here today? If not, we must conclude that something is wrong. We must seek the Lord's forgiveness for those areas where we have gone wrong. We must plead with him to show mercy, to come again to us in power, to revive his work, to build his church and demonstrate its unstoppable advance against the powers of hell.

PESTERING GOD: TWO PARABLES

Jesus told two parables which invite us to pester God about our need for the revival of the work of the gospel.

---

22. Passantino & Passantino, *Gates of Hell*, lines 53–56.

Luke 11:5-8

A friend turns up at your house at midnight, and you have no food indoors. You were planning to go shopping in the morning. But now here's your friend, hungry after a journey, and you've got nothing to give him for supper. What do you do? You pop next door and ask your neighbor if you could borrow three bread rolls. You'll replace them tomorrow, once you've been to Tesco. At least now you'll be able to make your friend a couple of sandwiches before he turns in. But your neighbor has already gone to bed, and he's not too impressed to be disturbed at such an unearthly hour. But, undeterred, you just keep on ringing his doorbell until, in desperation, he opens up and virtually throws a freezer full of bread at you.

In the parable Jesus commends your persistence. The word really means shamelessness, brazenness, brashness, impudence. That's what prevailed with the neighbor. Jesus then continues, "ask, and it will be given to you; seek, and you will find; knock, and it will be opened to you." (verse 9). The tense of the verbs he uses suggest that he is telling us to be just as impertinent when we pray, and he assures us in verse 10 that "everyone who asks receives, and he who seeks finds, and to him who knocks it will be opened." And the tense is the same. It is as we pray so persistently that we are becoming indecent that God takes notice. That's not because God is as reluctant to help us as the neighbor in the story. It's because when we pray with desperation, God knows that we mean business.

But this sort of praying is not just about any old thing. It's not that if we hammer at heaven's door, we can wangle out of God anything we like. Prayer is not about our preferences or fancies. Jesus' application follows in verse 13. He has pointed out how even sinful fathers don't taunt their children by giving them something dangerous. Then he continues: "If you then, being evil, know how to give good gifts to your children, how much more will your heavenly Father give the Holy Spirit to those who ask him!" It is prayer for the outpouring of the Holy Spirit that Jesus is talking about.

The friend in the story who arrived at midnight needed to be fed. We have friends, fellow human beings, who are hungering and thirsting for the bread of life. They may not be fully aware of that, but deep in their souls there is a sense of empty dissatisfaction that only Christ can fill. Left to ourselves, we can only say what the man in Jesus' parable said: "I have nothing to set before him." He had to go next door to get what he needed. We need the Holy Spirit if the work of feeding the multitudes with the nourishing truth of the gospel is to proceed effectively. Jesus is telling us to make sure that we are so desperately aware of our need, so urgently conscious of our helplessness, that nothing will stop us from asking, seeking, knocking, from pounding on heaven's door, until the Holy Spirit is poured out and the needy souls of men and women are fed with Christ's salvation.

Luke 18:1–8

Jesus told this story because he knows how easily we "lose heart" in prayer. The lesson of the parable is that "men always ought to pray and not lose heart." There are three characters in this story. The first is a widow. Her husband has died. As a result of the bereavement, she is left alone. She is lonely. The widow is a symbol of the church in days of decline. The Bible uses such a picture on two occasions. Isaiah 54:4 is addressed to God's people living through days of adversity, when their enemies seem to be in the ascendancy, and their numbers are greatly reduced compared with what they used to be. The prophet describes this as "the reproach of your widowhood." Jeremiah also uses this picture in Lamentations 1:1. Jerusalem has recently been overrun. Many of its citizens have been deported. The prophet laments, "How lonely sits the city that was full of people! How like a widow is she, who was great among the nations!" Perhaps we feel a bit like a widowed church today. The work of the gospel is not advancing in our land. Things seem to go from bad to worse to the very abyss. Some of us can remember rather better days in our youth. We can read of very much better days earlier in our national history. What has happened? The church is bereft. Our power has gone. Our numbers have declined. Our effectiveness is pretty poor. We are the widowed church.

The second character in the story is the adversary. He does not actually appear in person, but only by report. The widow in the parable is being harassed by someone who refuses to treat her fairly. Later in Luke Jesus refers to people "who devour widows houses" (Luke 20:47). We don't know exactly how they did this, but by some evil means or other these people exploited poor widows in order to enrich themselves and to leave the widows even more seriously impoverished. Well we too have an adversary, and he too is out to devour us. 1 Peter 5:8 tells us as much: "your adversary the devil walks about like a roaring lion, seeking whom he may devour." The word translated "adversary" here is the same as in Luke 18:3, and although the word for "devour" is not the same as in Luke 20:47, there is a connection. The word in Luke means to eat up; the word in Peter means to drink up. And our adversary, the devil, is actively devouring the church and its interests in our nation these days. Faith is weak. Apathy and hostility abound. Atheism prevails. Believers are nervous and fearful. Churches decline and close.

The third character is the judge. He's the kind of politician who's only in it for himself. He enjoys the prestige. It gives him a thrill to exercise power. Being judge is a brilliant opportunity to make a lot of money. He has neither moral commitment nor human compassion. He is "the unjust judge" (verse 6).

And now the three characters come together, as the widow appeals to the judge for justice against her adversary. To begin with he is not the least bit interested. Having to sort out petty things like this is just a nuisance. He'd rather be off to Rome administering the affairs of the empire, than listening to the trivial problems of one constituent. However, he soon discovered that irate widows could be an even greater nuisance. This widow just would not be put off. Every time the judge said, "No!" she simply returned the next day with the same request. Perhaps the bureaucracy of the day meant that he had to file a report in triplicate every time she turned up. And eventually she probably started coming both before and after lunch on the same day. Certainly the judge refers to "her continual coming." It was endless, and very taxing. The widow was troubling the judge, and he was getting weary. She really was overreaching herself. He felt as if he was being beaten black and blue, and he was getting fed up. So reluctantly he agreed to sort out the widow's problem just to get her off his back.

Jesus says in verse 6, "Hear what the unjust judge said." I think we are supposed to laugh at that point. Jesus is saying, Can you believe it! after everything he's said and done, he caves in before a poor widow! But the whole point is that the widowed church, buffeted by an adversary, crying out constantly, is not appealing to the deaf ear of an evil politician. God shall avenge his elect people, and speedily too. So we ought always to pray and not lose heart.

But someone might say, but we do pray and God ignores us. Our prayers don't get answered. I wonder. Jesus is telling us that it's when we "cry out night and day to him" (verse 7) that God heeds our appeal. That's not because he's as reluctant as the unjust judge, and so we've got to batter him into submission to us, and counteract his reluctance to hear us or help us. Rather, it's that when we cry to God out of a sense of pain and dire need, and when we do it night and day, when we really pester God with our cries for revival, that he knows that we are serious. Pestering praying reveals to God that we really are desperate, that we understand that we are helpless unless he does something, that our case is hopeless without his intervention. Careless, casual praying doesn't get answered, because it tells God that we're not that bothered, we don't really care about the reputation of his Son in the land.

That's why Jesus finishes verse 8 the way he does: "Nevertheless, when the Son of Man comes, will he really find faith on the earth?" If we read those words all on their own, we might think that Jesus is saying that by the time of his second coming there will be hardly any Christians in the world, that faith will virtually have died out. It gives us a picture of Jesus returning just in the nick of time, before his cause is completely lost. But that can't be what Jesus means. For one thing, it's totally inconsistent with the vision of Scripture as a whole, of the kingdom of God in Christ increasing constantly, until it fills the whole earth. For another thing, it hardly fits the immediate context, and would be totally irrelevant to this parable. Rather, these words are a challenge. They link back with the first verse. "Faith" is the same as not losing heart but always praying. When our faith wavers we give up on prayer. The coming Jesus mentions now is not his second, or, we might say, his final coming. He is talking about any occasion when he might come to us in our prayers, in his word, in our personal devotions, in our corporate worship, in our spiritual experience. What will he find when he comes? That's the challenge. Will he find hearts and churches so desperate to see his glory in the world, his honor restored in our land, his kingdom expanding invincibly, that we are crying out to God in earnest, urgent, believing prayer? Here is our New Testament mandate to pray for revival, to plead with God for that worldwide extension of Christ's kingdom, for the days of gospel glory, when the adversary will deceive the nations no more. Will we rise to the challenge?

JESUS' TRIUMPHAL ENTRY INTO JERUSALEM

A few days before his crucifixion Jesus rode into Jerusalem on the back of a donkey. In this event, the prophecy of Zechariah 9:9 was fulfilled. This verse is quoted in Matthew 21:5 and John 12:15. Here is another example of Old Testament prophecy being drawn by the inspired writers into the theology of the New Testament. Here is further evidence of the impossibility of constructing a New Testament theology of revival independently of the Old Testament.

Zechariah 9

Zechariah 9 begins by proclaiming God's judgment on Syria, represented by its capital city, Damascus, on Lebanon, the current name for the area containing the cities of Tyre and Sidon, and on Philistia, four of whose cities are named: Ashkelon, Gaza, Ekron, and Ashdod. These nations and cities were selected because they were neighbors of the people of God in Judah. However, they stand as representative Gentile nations. Their experience will be mirrored throughout the world. And Zechariah's point is that the judgment is not going to be total. Verse 7 speaks of a remnant from these nations who will belong to the God of Israel, who will become like one of the clans of Judah, and who will be like the Jebusites, who were incorporated into the kingdom of Israel after their conquest by David.

Here is a promise of the conversion of these Gentile peoples, and, indirectly, of all the Gentile nations of the world. Thomas Moore finds the initial fulfillment of this prophecy in Luke 6:17–18, which tells us of "a great multitude of people from all Judea and Jerusalem and from the seacoast of Tyre and Sidon, who came to hear him [Jesus] and be healed of their diseases." He also notes that many churches were planted along that coastline through the ministry of the apostle Paul.[23] But as the initial fulfillment, those New Testament texts point us onwards and forwards into later history as the kingdom of Christ extends to the ends of the earth. And that is the theme to which Zechariah now turns.

At verse 9, Zechariah's tone changes. The theme of judgment recedes into the background. This section begins with a call to rejoice, and that joy is bound up with the coming of Jesus, the Christ, the righteous and humble king. He comes, bringing with him a salvation which is not his exclusive possession, but which he carries as a gift for other people. Verse 10 indicates that Christ's peaceful reign is to be both exemplary and influential. Israel will no longer think of mounting a military campaign to rid itself of Gentile domination. Instead, war will become a relic of history. The influential reign of Christ will bring peace to the nations, as it extends to the ends of the earth. This worldwide peace will be the fruit of the conversion of the nations. Through the preaching of the gospel in the power

23. Moore, *Zechariah*, 143.

of the Holy Spirit, churches will be planted not only along the coastline of Lebanon, but in every nation on earth. Multitudes will come to Christ, not just from Tyre and Sidon, but from every city, town and village in the world. Gentile nations will be transformed by the power of the gospel, and Christ will be recognized worldwide as the rightful king over all. Moore comments: "We have only to patiently labor, and patiently wait, and the white banner of the lowly king shall in due time be unfurled from every mountain-top, and over every valley, and men be brother-murderers and brother-haters no more."[24]

Moore is certainly right to say that, in our day and generation we must patiently labor as we wait for the fulfillment of the prophecies of a worldwide day of glory for Jesus Christ, which will be achieved through the preaching of the glorious gospel. Since it is through the preaching of the gospel that it will be achieved, it is obvious that we must continue to labor in gospel work. I would add to Moore's comment the additional observation that we must patiently pray. Our gospel labors cannot bring in this worldwide revival on their own. Only the power of the Holy Spirit can accomplish the conversion of nation after nation, until the whole world is brought into submission to Christ. As we work, so we must pray, expressing our total dependence upon God, and our thoroughgoing expectancy that God will keep his promises.

Psalm 118:25–26

As Jesus rode into Jerusalem, the crowds celebrated his coming. Matthew 21:9 records that "the multitudes who went before him and those who followed cried out, saying, 'Hosanna to the Son of David! Blessed is he who comes in the name of the Lord! Hosanna in the highest!'" Luke 19:38 amplifies Matthew's statement a little, as he notes that the people recognized Christ's kingly majesty in this incident. They shouted, "Blessed is the King who comes in the name of the Lord!" Moreover, Luke fills out the meaning of Matthew's word "Hosanna," as he renders the final phrase, "Peace in heaven and glory in the highest!" Mark 11:9–10 omits the reference to Jesus as the Son of David after the initial "Hosanna," but adds, in the middle of the celebratory words, the phrase, "Blessed is the kingdom of our father David that comes in the name of the Lord!" In John 12:13, as in Mark,

---

24. Moore, *Zechariah*, 151.

the initial "Hosanna" stands alone, and after the words, "Blessed is he who comes in the name of the Lord," John adds, "the King of Israel!"

Behind the crowd's words there lies Psalm 118:25–26. The simple "Hosanna" found in Mark and John is equivalent to the opening words of verse 25, "save us, we pray." Matthew's addition "to the Son of David!" is typical of his gospel. In Matthew there are ten references to Jesus as the Son of David[25], compared with a combined total of just seven in Mark and Luke.[26] The term is not found in John's Gospel. It reflects the fact that the one who comes to save does so as the one in whom the covenant with David is fulfilled. He is the one who shall sit on the throne for ever. The phrase "Son of David" replaces the words "O Lord!" from the Psalm. Whereas the Psalmist invoked the Lord's salvation, the crowd in Jerusalem are voicing the conviction that the Lord has himself come to save in Jesus the Son of David.

The words, "blessed is he who comes in the name of the Lord" are taken directly from Psalm 118:26. In between the opening words of verse 25, "save us, we pray, O Lord," and these words, is the prayer, "O Lord, I pray, send prosperity." The word rendered "prosperity" contains the idea of a speedy advance. Although it was omitted by the crowd in Jerusalem on Palm Sunday, their use of these verses, as cited by the Gospel writers, compels us to read their significance in the light of the surrounding phrases which are applied to Christ. And since the words are strictly speaking a prayer, they show us, in summary form, what the content and burden of our prayers ought to be. This is our prayer for revival—that God would prosper the kingdom of his Son, that he would send the gospel rapidly and successfully to every corner of the globe. Since this is a divinely inspired prayer, we may confidently expect to see Christ's kingdom speedily advancing through the world, his gospel rapidly progressing, and achieving success. Christ's great work is not going to peter out and come to nothing, or even to next to nothing. The world must be brought into his kingdom. He must triumph obviously in the present age.

The variations on the opening sentence of Psalm 118:26 found in the Gospels are also instructive and encouraging as we pray for revival. Luke simply replaces the word "he" with "the King." John adds to the Psalmist's original words a note to the effect that Jesus is "the King of Israel." This assures us that the one who is to see unrivaled success throughout the world

---

25. Matt 1:1, 20; 9:27; 12:23; 15:22; 20:30–31; 21:9, 15; 22:42.

26. Mark 10:47–48; 12:35; Luke 3:31; 18:38–39; 20:41.

truly is the world's proper king, and as such he shall prosper. It is indeed his *kingdom* that will progress rapidly. John's wording confirms that Jesus Christ is appointed king by the God of Israel, the only true God, and that this guarantees the successful expansion of his kingdom. The gospel prosperity anticipated by the Psalmist is seen in the increasing evidence of the reign of Jesus Christ over all the nations. Mark especially emphasizes this when he replaces the reference to the king with a mention of the kingdom itself. At this point he inserts a reference to David, affirming that it is as the one to whom the promises are given that Jesus comes and reigns and prospers. All the Old Testament promises to David are therefore taken up in these words, and we must look expectantly for the faithful Father's fulfillment of his word.

Jesus alludes to this Psalm again in the context of his parable about the wicked vinedressers (Matthew 21:42; Mark 12:10; Luke 20:17). This time he quotes verses 22–23 of the Psalm: "The stone which the builders rejected has become the chief cornerstone. This was the LORD's doing, and it is marvelous in our eyes." Luke cites only verse 22. Reading these words in the light of the following verses and their use in the New Testament reminds us that Jesus is the chief cornerstone as the one whose kingdom prospers throughout the world.

Psalm 148:1

The final part of the crowd's chant as Jesus rode into Jerusalem is possibly an allusion to Psalm 148:1: "Praise the LORD! Praise the LORD from the heavens; praise him in the heights!" The final phrase of this verse, "in the heights," is identical in the Septuagint to the words of the Greek text of Matthew 21:9 translated "in the highest." If this is the background, then the praise being offered by the Jerusalem crowds is specifically for the LORD's saving work, for that is the meaning of "Hosanna." That saving work is even now coming to its climax and focus in Christ, as he goes towards the cross.

Luke's variant, "peace in heaven and glory in the highest," seems to be an intentional echo of the song that the angels sang the night that Christ was born: "Glory to God in the highest, and on earth peace, good will toward men" (Luke 2:14). Then, they sang "peace on earth." Now the crowd shouts, "peace in heaven." The work of Christ establishes peace on earth. Sinners are brought to peace with God, and the universal reign of Christ will usher in an era of peace for the world. And it is when the gospel message, proclaimed in the power of the Spirit, brings these expressions of peace into being, that heaven itself is at peace. The sense is that God is restless as long as sinners are unsaved and the nations are in turmoil because of the power of sin and the domination of the devil. When peace comes to earth through Christ, when sinners are saved, and when the devil's deceptive power is nullified, then heaven too finds peace. God rejoices over the salvation of the lost. What a mandate, then, the New Testament gives us to pray for global revival, for the establishment of Christ's kingdom, in the confident certainty that the Father must keep the promises he has made to his Son.

THE CLEANSING OF THE TEMPLE

As Jesus was driving out the traders who had set up their stalls in the temple, he quoted two Old Testament Scriptures. Matthew 21:13 (cf. Luke 19:46) reads,

> He said to them, "It is written, 'My house shall be called a house of prayer,' but you have made it a 'den of thieves.'"

The first quotation, "My house shall be called a house of prayer," comes from Isaiah 56:7, and the words "a den of thieves" from Jeremiah 7:11. Mark 11:17 enlarges on the first quotation: "My house shall be called a house of prayer for all nations." Actually, both Mark's wording and that of Matthew and Luke are taken from the Isaiah text, which in fact contains both phrases:

> Even them I will bring to my holy mountain, and make them joyful in my house of prayer. Their burnt offerings and their sacrifices will be accepted on my altar; for my house shall be called a house of prayer for all nations.

This text is particularly relevant for our present theme. The opening words, "even them I will bring," points us back to the preceding verse in order to identify the people denoted by the word "them." We discover that they are "the sons of the foreigner who join themselves to the LORD, to serve him, and to love the name of the LORD, to be his servants." They have in fact been part of the topic of discussion since verse 3, and verse 5 begins similarly to verse 7: "even to them." The message of verses 3–5 is that those who have been shut out from the congregation of Israel, such as the sons of the foreigner, and eunuchs, when they join themselves to the LORD and demonstrate the reality of that by choosing a lifestyle which pleases the LORD, will certainly not be second class citizens within the people, the kingdom, the family of God. Isaiah is anticipating the day when Gentile foreigners will be converted. Through the prophet, "the Lord GOD, who gathers the outcasts of Israel, says, 'Yet I will gather to him others besides those who are gathered to him'" (verse 8), and the phrase which Mark selects out of verse 7 indicates that they will come from all nations. Through Isaiah God says, "I will . . . make them joyful in my house of prayer." That is the fruit of the gospel—sinners reveling in their salvation, nations celebrating the grace of God in Christ, the entire world erupting with gospel joy as the kingdom of Christ exerts its global influence, and reduces all rival powers to nothing. This is a purpose which cannot fail, because it is the LORD who does the gathering. Until the gospel has made this impact on all the nations, therefore, we must continue to pray for that worldwide outpouring of the Spirit.

Matthew goes on to tell us that, while Jesus is still in the temple, the children repeat the cry of the crowd on Palm Sunday, "Hosanna to the Son of David." The indignant priests ask Jesus whether he is aware of what the children are saying. In reply, Jesus quotes Psalm 8:2: "Out of the mouth of babes and nursing infants you have perfected praise" (Matthew 21:15–16). Psalm 8 celebrates the excellence of the LORD's name in all the earth, and the fact that he has crowned man with glory and honor, and entrusted him with dominion over the whole creation. Hebrews 2:5–9 makes it clear that this Psalm, in its ultimate meaning, is not talking about any and every man, or mankind as a race, but about one specific man, Jesus Christ. He is the one to whom total and global dominion is given. The result of his worldwide triumph is that the excellence of the LORD's name will truly be recognized everywhere. That is what we must pray for. That is the worldwide revival, which the New Testament encourages us to expect.

DAVID'S SON AND DAVID'S LORD

One day Jesus posed a conundrum for the Pharisees. He asked them whose son the Messiah was to be. They rightly responded, "The son of David." He then asked them how the Messiah could be David's son, when David himself called him his Lord. Jesus then quoted Psalm 110:1, "The LORD said to my Lord, 'Sit at my right hand, till I make your enemies your footstool.'" They were flummoxed, but Jesus' point was to assert his dual nature as man and God. Only thus could he be both David's son and David's Lord (Matthew 22:41–46; Mark 12:35–37; Luke 20:41–44).

However, the fact that Jesus used this text means that he is claiming to be the true fulfillment of David's prophetic vision in that Psalm. And the vision is of the total victory of the kingdom of the Messiah, who is both king and priest. Here again we see how it is impossible to read the New Testament in isolation from the Old Testament. By Jesus' words, Psalm 110 is drawn into the New Testament theology of revival. Following Jesus' lead, other New Testament passages also interpret this Psalm as a prophecy about Jesus, in particular his ascension (e.g., Acts 2:34). We shall focus on the first three verses of this Psalm.

Verse 1 contains a solemn promise made by the Father to the Son: "The LORD said to my Lord, 'Sit at my right hand, till I make your enemies your footstool.'" The word "said" here is really a bit tame. This verb is only ever used of a word of God. At three o'clock on the afternoon of every Christmas Day, the announcement is made over our televisions and radios, "Her Majesty speaks to the Commonwealth." We are prepared for a notable address by the monarch. That, only more so, is the significance of the verb "said" in Psalm 110:1. It is not just any old piece of chat. It refers to an awesome statement, a great speech, a formidable promise.

And what the God the Father promises God the Son is complete victory. That is what is implied in the idea of his enemies becoming his footstool. The imagery reflects Joshua 10:24. Joshua has just led the Israelite army to victory over five Amorite kings. Now he instructs his captains, "put your feet on the necks of these kings." It continues, "they drew near and put their feet on their necks." This symbolized their total defeat. All Christ's enemies face total defeat on the strength of the Father's promise.

The second line of Psalm 110:2 reads, "Rule in the midst of your enemies!" The word translated "rule" is taken from Genesis 1:26 and 28, where it speaks of human dominion over all God's earthly works. Its recurrence here suggests that Christ's complete victory will mean that everything is back as it was at the beginning, everything exactly as it was supposed to be all along.

The first line of verse 2 shows us how Christ's complete victory will take place: "The LORD shall send the rod of your strength out of Zion." The best known pair of rods in the Bible belonged to Moses and Aaron. Moses' rod was twice called "the rod of God" (Exodus 4:20; 17:9). But this rod was symbolic. God spoke, Moses stretched out his rod, then what God had said happened. Here is just one example. The seventh of the judgments on Egypt was the devastating hailstorm. In Exodus 9:18 the LORD speaks: "tomorrow about this time I will cause very heavy hail to rain down, such as has not been in Egypt since its founding until now." Then verse 23 tells us, "Moses stretched out his rod toward heaven; and the LORD sent thunder and hail, and fire darted to the ground. And the LORD rained hail on the land of Egypt." The rod represented the word of God. We may sum up God's word for today as the gospel message. That is the rod by which Jesus' complete victory will be achieved.

The Psalm speaks of this gospel rod as "the rod of your strength." The word translated "strength" is derived from a verb meaning "to prevail." So the gospel is Christ's prevailing rod, his winning rod. Moses' and Aaron's rods were winning rods. There was that time when Aaron threw his rod on the ground and it turned into a serpent. The magicians of Egypt did the same thing, but then Aaron's rod swallowed up all the others (Exodus 7:10–12). There was the occasion when the Israelites were grumbling about the leadership of Moses and Aaron. God said that he would demonstrate whom he had chosen for leadership amongst his people. He instructed the leader of each tribe to take a rod and place them in the tabernacle. The next morning Aaron's rod had budded (Numbers 17:1–8). On these two occasions, Aaron's rod was the winning rod. Then there was the time when Israel was fighting the Amalekites. As long as Moses held his rod up high, Israel prevailed. As his arms grew tired, he needed help to keep his rod lifted up, but in the end "Joshua defeated Amalek and his people with the edge of the sword" (Exodus 17:9–13). So Moses' rod was the winning rod.

In today's intellectual climate there are many competing messages vying for supremacy. There is the rod of evolutionism, the rod of political correctness, the rod of Islam, the rod of pluralism, the rod of gay liberation, the rod of atheism. But however strong these rods may seem to be, we know without a shadow of doubt that the rod of the gospel is going to win.

Verse 3 explains why this is so. This victory is achieved because the rod of the gospel proves to have such an amazing, transforming effect on the lives of those who embrace it: "your people shall be volunteers in the day of your power, in the beauties of holiness." I think that is how the verse should be punctuated, with the main break at this point. To speak of Christ's people as "volunteers" is an amazing statement, because, by nature, everyone of them is an enemy, a rebel, a sinner. Yet the power of the gospel is to turn enemies into happy friends, to turn rebels into loyal subjects. The gospel changes people who were once foolishly captivated by the fleeting and spurious pleasures of sin into lovers of "the beauties of holiness."

The word rendered "volunteers" is normally translated "freewill offerings." Through the gospel believers make freewill offerings of themselves. We may note three characteristics of a freewill offering. It was offered from a willing heart that wanted to obey the LORD's commands (Exodus 35:29). It was offered continuously (Exodus 36:3). It was offered in grateful response for God's blessing (Deuteronomy 16:10). When we believe the gospel and repent of our sins, our hearts become eager to obey God continuously. And this is not some self-motivated act, by which we seek to ingratiate ourselves with God. Rather, we say, Since you, Lord, have done so much in Christ for me, how I can want to do anything other than give myself freely to you?

The Psalm tells us that this gospel victory in the lives of sinners takes place in the day of Christ's power. In the New Testament power is often associated with the Holy Spirit. For example, Jesus said, "you shall receive power when the Holy Spirit has come upon you" (Acts 1:8). Paul writes like this to the Thessalonians: "our gospel did not come to you in word only, but also in power, and in the Holy Spirit" (1 Thessalonians 1:5). The day of Christ's power is any time when the Holy Spirit is at work. In view of the Father's promise to his Son in this Psalm, we may legitimately expect a day when this power is seen at work simultaneously in every place. That is why there is most certainly a New Testament mandate to pray for the global outpouring of the Spirit, to pray for a worldwide revival which will not bypass any nation anywhere.

The second part of Psalm 110:3 is often described as "obscure." It says, "from the womb of the morning you have the dew of your youth." It seems to mean that, just as the dew is replenished every morning, so Christ's kingdom will come repeatedly in every generation, so that it never grows old, but is always fresh and flourishing, until that day when the entire world has been brought under the rule of Christ.

There is one phrase which we have not yet commented on. It is found in verse 2, "out of Zion." We are told that it is from Zion that the winning rod of the gospel will be sent forth. Zion in the Bible is a picture of the church of Jesus Christ. That is why Hebrews 12:22 can say to believers, "you have come to Mount Zion and to the city of the living God, the heavenly Jerusalem." This is not talking about heaven itself, because it is not true that we have already come there. It is speaking of the church as the earthly outpost of heaven. This is the Zion from which the gospel rod extends. This reminds us of one very vital thing. Praying for revival is not something which so takes over that we do nothing else. As we pray we also preach. We proclaim the gospel, we stretch out the rod, and we pray that God will use it to bring about Christ's complete victory in the present world. If we ever make praying for revival an alternative to gospel service we are in trouble. We are simply using intercession as an excuse for idleness. That is not a proper emphasis. Praying and gospel proclamation must always go hand-in-hand.

THE CROSS

It is probably true to say that the two most famous of Jesus' seven sayings from the cross are the cry of dereliction, "My God, my God, why have you forsaken me?" (Matthew 27:46; Mark 15:34), and the triumphant shout, "It is finished" (John 19:30).

In the cry of dereliction Jesus quotes the opening words of Psalm 22. The Psalm goes on to portray Jesus' crucifixion and the surrounding events in very vivid terms. Although John does not quote this cry, he, along with Matthew, does quote another verse from Psalm 22. All four Gospel writers tell of how the soldiers shared out Jesus' clothes and cast lots for his tunic (Matthew 27:35; Mark 15:24; Luke 23:34; John 19:23–24). Matthew and John note that this was explicitly predicted in Psalm 22:18: "They divide my garments among them, and for my clothing they cast lots."

But even where Psalm 22 is not directly quoted there are enough echoes of its words in the Gospel accounts of the crucifixion to indicate that this Psalm clearly prophesies the sufferings of Christ. Verses 6–8 clearly anticipate the mockery which Jesus faced as he hung on the cross (Matthew 27:39–43; Mark 15:29–32; Luke 23:35–37). Verses 12–13 glance back at Jesus' arrest, and his trials before the Jewish leaders and the Roman governor, when he was surrounded by enemies baying for his blood. The simile in verse 14, "I am poured out like water," reminds us of the words of John 19:34: "One of the soldiers pierced his side with a spear, and immediately blood and water came out." The references to the sufferer's bones in verses 14 and 17, disjointed, yet all present and unbroken, remind us of another incident which John reports. The Jews requested that the legs of the three victims be broken to hasten their deaths. So the soldiers broke the legs of the two criminals on either side of Jesus, "but when they came to Jesus and saw that he was already dead, they did not break his legs" (John 19:31–33).

John again notes that this was a fulfillment of the Scripture which said, "Not one of his bones shall be broken" (John 19:36). This is not an exact quotation of any particular passage, but an echo of several Old Testament Scriptures, and it is quite possible that John had Psalm 22:17 in mind in addition to other texts.

Then verse 15 is a direct prediction of the thirst with which Jesus would be afflicted as he hung there exposed to the midday heat (John 19:28). The words of verse 16, "they pierced my hands and my feet," point on to several New Testament texts. The word "pierced" comes in John's account of the crucifixion in connection with the piercing of Jesus' side with the spear (John 19:34, 37). John uses it again in a more general way in Revelation 1:7. The fact that nails pierced Jesus' hands and feet is clear from the way in which he pointed to his hands and feet as evidence of his identity after his resurrection (Luke 24:39–40; cf. John 20:20), and from Thomas's words in John 20:25, "Unless I see in his hands the print of the nails, and put my finger into the print of the nails, and put my hand into his side, I will not believe."

As Jesus quoted Psalm 22:1 and uttered the cry of dereliction, he had reached his lowest point. The weight of the world's sin crushed him. The outpouring of the wrath of God was torturing his soul. It was at that moment, if at all, that he descended into hell, as the creed puts it.

However, the Psalm's description of crucifixion is interspersed with affirmations of confidence in the very God who has now forsaken his Son, and then the whole Psalm ends on a note of triumph. We may be sure that Jesus, even as he quoted the opening words, had the entire context in his mind and heart, and was gazing through the pain to the glories beyond. In fact, it is often suggested that when Jesus "said, 'It is finished!'" (John 19:30), he was consciously alluding to the final phrase of this Psalm, "he has done this" (Psalm 22:31). It was a shout of victory, celebrating the fact that, in his suffering and death, God had accomplished his purpose.

And what is the purpose which God has achieved through the crucifixion of his Son? Verses 27–28 of Psalm 22 sum it up. It is that "all the ends of the world . . . and all the families of the nations" should "turn to the LORD," becoming his worshippers, because the kingdom rule over all the nations belongs to him. Verse 29 teaches that all ranks of society shall be blessed in Christ, and verses 30–31 indicate the fulfillment of this purpose for all generations. This is the prize which the Lord Jesus Christ receives because of his obedience to death. This is his reward for the agony of his

God-forsakenness. The world will be his. The kingdom of God in history will be entrusted to him. And the key defining feature of Christ's reign will be satisfaction (verse 26). Those in dire spiritual need shall find all their hopes fulfilled in Christ.

So if we do not yet see all the ends of the world impacted by the gospel, we must plead these promises. If we do not yet see every family in every nation blessed by the message of Christ, we must pray for the fulfillment of God's purpose. If we see segments of society still unreached, we have a mandate to pray for the complete penetration of gospel power. If we live in a generation where apostasy and unbelief dominate, we are duty-bound to cry to the Lord for his mercy in our time. And by quoting the opening words of this Psalm, and then alluding to its final words, our Lord and Savior himself draws the vision and promises of Psalm 22 into a New Testament theology of revival.

THE GREAT COMMISSION

We are familiar with the use of Christ's great commission as a challenge to missionary service. But perhaps we are less clear than we should be about the promises, explicit and implied, within the commission. We ought not to overlook these, as they are the source of our motivation for obedience to the commission.

In Mark's version of the great commission Jesus says, "Go into all the world and preach the gospel to every creature" (Mark 16:15). Luke tells us of the occasion when he said to the disciples "that repentance and remission of sins should be preached in his name to all nations" (Luke 24:47). Two things claim our attention here.

The first is the verb "preach," used in both these texts. The word speaks of a proclamation which takes place with authority, and which must be obeyed. It is linked with the word for a herald. Lothar Coenen makes the following comments about the role of the herald in Greek society. The herald served under the authority of his master. He had no liberty of his own to negotiate. He had to announce his master's message intact, and what he announced became valid by the act of proclamation. His proclamation was a binding command, and was not merely the making of an offer or the imparting of information.[27] Surely the choice of this word implies that Jesus expected that the gospel command, issued under his supreme authority,

27. Coenen, "*kērussō*," 49–50.

would be effective. The very proclamation of the gospel will result in its impact upon every place where it is preached. The call to repent will not prove to be a mere suggestion or offer. The promise of forgiveness will not come across merely as a piece of academic information. The promise of forgiveness will result in people actually being forgiven. The call to repentance will result in people truly repenting everywhere where the heralded message goes. We must expect nothing less. There is no place for pessimism or disillusionment in gospel work. There is every reason for maximum expectation. The success of the gospel is guaranteed.

The second thing to note is the reference to "all the world" in Mark, and "all nations" in Luke. This is the scope of that proclamation with guaranteed effectiveness. No nation is to be left untouched. The whole world will feel the impact of the gospel. That is what our Lord has promised.

Three things follow. The first is that we must believe the word of God. We have become such despondent people. We have been overcome by the idea that the gospel is a lost cause. We have started to think of decline and ineffectiveness as normal, and lost our expectancy. We have ceased to believe the word of God, because we have allowed contemporary appearances in our small corner of the world to daunt us. This ought not to be so! God's word should shape our anticipation. Secondly, given that the gospel is not advancing with mighty power in our part of the world today, that fact should be impeling us to fervent, constant prayer. We must not settle for the idea that this is normal and it will never be any different. Rather, the very abnormality of the situation should catapult us into concerted prayer that God will fulfill his word. Thirdly, the great commission reminds us that we are not just to sit back and wait for it all to happen. If the promise of Jesus is to be fulfilled, there is something that we must do. We must be serving as heralds. We must be preaching the gospel to all nations. We must be calling men and women to repentance, and announcing the forgiveness of sins which will follow. This is not because Jesus is impotent without our help! It is because he graciously invites us to become sharers with him in the worldwide extension of his kingdom, until the day when his reign on earth by his word is manifestly obvious in every nation simultaneously.

It is the version of the great commission which Matthew gives us which is the fullest, and probably the most well known. Here are Jesus words to his disciples on the mountain in Galilee:

> All authority has been given to me in heaven and on earth. Go
> therefore and make disciples of all the nations, baptizing them in

the name of the Father and of the Son and of the Holy Spirit, teaching them to observe all that I have commanded you; and lo, I am with you always, even to the end of the age (Matthew 28:18–20).

Once again the command is there to go to all the nations. The commission is to make disciples, and the following clauses are the fuller definition of what that means. Discipleship begins with baptism, the symbol of conversion and the life-changing commitment involved. Discipleship continues as a lifelong process of learning and obeying all that Jesus has commanded.

But we must notice Jesus' exact words, "make disciples of all the nations." What is the significance of the word "of"? The English rendering could be taken to mean "make some disciples out of all the nations," but that is not exactly what the words seem to mean in the original language. "Make disciples of" is all one word in Greek. It could be translated, "disciple all the nations." "All the nations" is the direct object of the verb "disciple." In other words, Jesus could be read as meaning that it is the nations themselves that are to be the target of the church's discipling mission, not just individuals from all the nations. Again, the implication seems to be that through the preaching of the gospel entire nations will be discipled in the way of Christ. That is to say, the nations as such are to be brought under the authority of Christ.

Such an expectation is voiced in the words of one verse of the hymn, *O Spirit of the living God*. The fifth verse goes like this:

Baptize the nations; far and nigh
The triumphs of the cross record:
The name of Jesus glorify,
Till every kindred call him Lord.[28]

It is, of course, true that this happens as individuals from all the nations are converted, baptized, and taught. You cannot literally baptize a nation as such. Nevertheless, the goal which we must always be aiming at is the discipleship of nations in their entirety. The goal is the total transformation of culture in every land on earth, such that every nation lives by the light of the word of God, from the highest political leaders to the humblest member of society. Nothing short of a worldwide impact of scriptural truth can satisfy the promise implicit in Jesus' words. That should always be the thrust of our intercession and our evangelism.

---

28. By James Montgomery, 1771–1854.

Matthew Henry defines "the principal intention of this commission" like this: "do your utmost to make the nations Christian nations." Then he elaborates on this vision: "Christ the Mediator is setting up a kingdom in the world, bring the nations to be his subjects; setting up a school, bring the nations to be his scholars; raising an army for the carrying on of the war against the powers of darkness, enlist the nations of the earth under his banner."[29]

It is the fact that Jesus possesses authority over everything which justifies us in working for biblical principles in every sphere of society, in protesting against error being taught in schools, paraded in the media, and assumed by the culture. Jesus is to be obeyed, and no person and no nation is exempt from that requirement.

29. Henry, *New Testament*, Vol. 2, 307–8.

3

THE TEACHING ON REVIVAL IN THE BOOK OF ACTS

INTRODUCTION

The book of Acts highlights the desperate situation which we are in to-day by way of contrast. At the same time it holds before us the realistic expectation that things will not always be the way we are experiencing them just now. I am assuming that the book of Acts describes the situation which we ought to regard as normal. God's word shows us how things should be. If the situation we are facing is different from the story told in Acts, then that means that today's situation is abnormal. We should therefore expect things to change and we should pray for things to change. The book of Acts certainly motivates us to cry out to God for revival.

There are some people who would protest that the events described in Acts were unique and extraordinary, that Acts is not at all a charter of expectancy for the church at all times and in all places. Now, it is certainly true that some things described in Acts were specific to that era and to particular places. However, to those who object that everything in Acts is in the category of the unique and extraordinary, I would ask this question: if the word of God is not our criterion for discovering what is normal, then where do we find the authoritative description of normality? If we assume that Acts describes an extraordinary state of affairs, and that the decline and ineffectiveness which we see today is normal, then are we not guilty of subjecting the word of God to our experience, and making our experience normative? That is precisely the method of liberal theology, and we should have nothing to do with it. God's word is normative, and we must always read our circumstances and our experience in the light of God's inspired revelation, and not vice versa. Maybe it is valid to say that the situation described in Acts is extraordinary, but that is only because normality for God is the extraordinary and extraordinary works are normal. God simply does not have the ability to do anything less than the extraordinary: he "only does wondrous things!" (Psalm 72:18).

Our problem is that we have become so used to decline and ineffectiveness that we have lost our expectancy. We have given way to unbelief. We have become despondent and negative in our attitudes. We bemoan the state of things, but the tone of our voice and the shrug of our shoulders betray the fact that we have resigned ourselves to it, and that we have no faith to cry out to the Lord for his dramatic intervention.

At this point I must acknowledge my debt to Albert Barnes for my understanding of the book of Acts. In his introduction to Acts Barnes summarizes "the design and importance" of the history which it tells.[1] He sees the book as "an inspired account of the character of true revivals." Barnes defines a revival as a remarkable display of divine power and mercy. Moreover, Barnes insists, in my view correctly, that regular revivals are to be expected. He takes it as a lesson from Acts that it will ordinarily be by Holy Spirit revivals that the preaching of the gospel will be blessed. The normal mode by which the gospel will spread and finally triumph among the nations throughout the world will be through outpourings of the Holy Spirit.

Additionally, Barnes makes the point that the church came into being solely by the clear and simple preaching of the truth, centered in the death and resurrection of Jesus Christ. Such preaching may expect to be attended with the influences of the Holy Spirit. Barnes finds in Acts a picture of the spirit of genuine Christianity. The gospel had to be preached to all nations, and anything that stood in the way of fulfilling that task had to be sacrificed. When necessary, toil and danger were to be suffered. Even death itself was cheerfully to be met if it would promote the spread of the gospel. As a result, within thirty years the gospel had spread to many parts of the world. Acts tells of its triumphs in Arabia, Asia Minor, Africa and Europe. Churches were already established in the great cities of the Roman Empire. And this happened in spite of tremendous opposition, and despite the fact

1. Barnes, *Acts*, iv–vii.

that the instruments were, for the most part, uneducated Jews. The explanation, Barnes says, is "they were taught only by the Holy Spirit, armed only with the power of God, victorious only because Christ was their captain." The success of the apostles in those years is conclusive evidence that the Christian faith is indeed God-given.

Barnes's references to sacrifice, toil, danger, opposition, and death deserve to be noticed. I fear that sometimes prayer for revival can be motivated by the discomfort of living in an alien environment. We imagine that, if only revival would come, life would be so much more pleasant for Christian people. The danger in this is that prayer for revival can simply become a religious expression of our natural, sinful selfishness. We lose the proper motivation which should only ever be concern for the honor of the name of the Lord. The fact is that true revival will not necessarily bring comfort and ease. It may come hand-in-hand with intense persecution. But if the Lord's name is exalted as a result, that is all that matters. Who do I think I am, to worry about my own comfort?

What, then, do we discover as we read the book of Acts? The answer in a nutshell is that the gospel makes a massive impact. Let's trace that impact through the book, pausing as we go to look in more detail at some key passages.

THE MASSIVE IMPACT OF THE GOSPEL

The impact began on the Day of Pentecost, when three thousand people were converted as a result of Peter's sermon (Acts 2:41). From then on there were daily additions to the Christian church (Acts 2:47). That is a phenomenon we are not seeing today. There is something we ought to be praying for in connection with revival.

The Impact in Jerusalem

Acts 3 and 4 recount the healing of the lame man who used to beg at the gateway into the temple courtyard. Such events were God's endorsement of the gospel as it began its progress around the world. When the man was healed a crowd gathered, and Peter took the opportunity to preach the gospel to them. But now, enter "the priests, the captain of the temple, and the Sadducees" (Acts 4:1). The gospel does not make progress without opposition. We must not fall into the trap of imagining that revival will spell the end of all our problems. When God is at work in mighty power, the opponents of Christ will rise in hostility.

The following day the apostles are brought before the leaders for questioning. After being asked for their authority for what they were doing and saying (verse 7), they simply preach Christ again with great boldness (verses 10–13). The leaders then threaten them, demanding that they speak no more in the name of Jesus. They politely indicate that they are unable to comply with this request. However, since the massive impact of the gospel is undeniable, there is nothing else that the leaders can do. As a result of this incident another few thousand people were added to the church. Acts 4:4 tells us that the number of men alone, not counting women at this point, had reached five thousand. If the number of women was similar, the total membership of the Christian congregations in Jerusalem by this time must have been in excess of ten thousand. And it is only a matter of days, or at the most a few weeks, since Pentecost! The huge number of converts now present in Jerusalem inevitably made an undeniable impact on the city as a whole. The entire population was aware of the notable miracle (Acts 4:16). So Peter and John have to be released.

They then report back to the church what has happened, and the church immediately unites in prayer (Acts 4:23–24). Here is our example for days of opposition and threatening. We must lift our voice to God in united prayer.

What we have in verses 24–30 is probably a summary of the gist of the prayers. My guess is that one after another led the assembled company to God in prayer, and they all united by joining in with a hearty "Amen" at the end of each prayer. Luke has summarized the general import of all the prayers. This shows that when we unite in prayer with an agreed common purpose, the entire prayer meeting is really a single prayer, and each person's prayer is a contribution to the total common prayer. We always have to remember that to listen with concentration to another praying and then to say "Amen" is to pray.

And so the steady stream of conversions continued. Acts 5:14 tells us that "believers were increasingly added to the Lord, multitudes of both men and women." The following chapter begins with a note that "the number of disciples was multiplying" (Acts 6:1), and verse 7 tells us that, as the days and months went by, continuously "the word of God spread, and the number of the disciples multiplied greatly in Jerusalem." Even some of those who had been the chief opponents were subdued by the preaching of the gospel: "a great many of the priests were obedient to the faith."

And it was the same in other places where the gospel was preached.

The Impact in Samaria

From Acts 8 we learn of Philip's ministry. Through him, the massive impact of gospel was felt in Samaria, where, "the multitudes with one accord heeded the things spoken by Philip" (Acts 8:6). We today can hardly secure a hearing for the gospel, let alone persuade people to believe it. When we read of crowds unitedly paying attention and taking note of the message, as they did in Samaria, we are challenged to pray for the same massive impact of the gospel in our generation.

Before the coming of the gospel, a magician called Simon had captivated the hearts of the Samaritans. Acts 8:10 says that "they all gave heed" to Simon, "from the least to the greatest." But then we read in verse 12, that "they believed Philip as he preached the things concerning the kingdom of God and the name of Jesus Christ." The word "they" in this verse refers to the same people as in verse 10. Everyone, "from the least to the greatest," now turned their attention to the message of Christ. Simon himself made a profession of faith (verse 13). However, the sequel indicates that in times of revival there will be some who are hangers-on, but who are not genuinely converted. At such times the fashionable, respectable thing is to identify with the Christian cause. This is regrettable, but probable. It encourages us to pray that all who profess the name of Christ will be soundly saved.

The Impact in the Desert

After his encouraging time in Samaria the Lord leads Philip into the desert. There he meets the Ethiopian eunuch and leads him to Christ (Acts 8:26–39). I think we can learn two lessons from this part of Philip's story.

The Removal of the Instrument

First, it may be necessary for those who have been used by the Holy Spirit as instruments of revival to be removed from the scene fairly soon. We have a natural tendency to pride. It is part of our sinful nature to want to take some of the glory for ourselves. However, God assures us, "I will not give my glory to another" (Isaiah 48:11; cf. Isaiah 42:8). It may well be safer for a gospel preacher who has been used in a time of revival to move to a new place, lest he fall into the temptation of claiming the credit for himself, of trying to tie his own name to the revival.

The Conversion of the Individual

Second, although revival results in numerous conversions at once, or in a short space of time, every conversion is the salvation of a single individual. Many people may come to Christ together, but each one must come personally. The conversion of one man in the desert is no less spectacular a miracle than the conversion of multitudes in the city. And all those who are saved in the city must believe for themselves in exactly the same way as the one in the desert. In revival, crowds are drawn to Christ simultaneously. But the world's population does not consist only of crowds in the cities. The more isolated rural areas also need the gospel. They are also part of the inheritance promised to Christ. When revival impacts the urban masses, its overspill will be a work of grace, inevitably smaller, but just as wonderful, amongst the dispersed individuals in adjoining areas. In our passion for revival, we must not so pursue the massive numbers in the major towns that we overlook the less densely populated places.

In Acts 9:31, we have one of Luke's occasional summaries. He notes that

> the churches throughout all Judea, Galilee, and Samaria had peace
> and were edified. And walking in the fear of the Lord and in the
> comfort of the Holy Spirit, they were multiplied.

This was one offshoot of the conversion of Saul of Tarsus.

The Impact on the Enemies of the Church

In days of revival the church's worst enemies suddenly find themselves overpowered by Christ, and totally transformed. That is the lesson which we derive from the account of Saul's conversion in Acts 9:1–19. A man who had devoted his life to destroying the church of Jesus Christ is confronted by Christ himself, and becomes an ardent advocate of the very gospel which he previously despised, so that the Judean believers can exclaim, "he who formerly persecuted us now preaches the faith which he once tried to destroy" (Galatians 1:23).

No doubt Saul had heard the gospel many times. He was familiar with its teaching. Now, as he travels towards Damascus, the Holy Spirit uses the word which has lodged in his mind, and Saul encounters the risen Jesus. Today we ought to pray especially for people like Richard Dawkins, for the governments of the remaining Communist nations, for the leaders of the various Islamic communities. When God's Spirit moves in revival power, we may confidently expect to see significant conversions amongst such people. Let us pray that, one way or another, they may hear the gospel, that the words which they hear will lodge in their memories, that the Holy Spirit will use the word to make Christ a living reality to them, that they will be converted, and that Christ's people may be multiplied.

The Impact in Other Cities

The story of the massive impact of the gospel in specific cities now resumes. The restoration of Dorcas to life "became known throughout all Joppa, and many believed on the Lord." (Acts 9:42). Clearly Peter took the opportunity while there to preach Christ. Syrian Antioch is in view in Acts 11:21 and 24, where we read these twin statements: "a great number believed and turned to the Lord, and a great many people were added to the Lord." The same thing happened in Tyre and Sidon: "the word of God grew and multiplied" (Acts 12:24).

Paul's evangelism was equally effective. In Pisidian Antioch we hear of people begging to hear the gospel. Acts 13:42 says that "the Gentiles begged that these words might be preached to them the next Sabbath." When that day came, "almost the whole city came together to hear the word of God": "multitudes" were gathering under the sound of the gospel (verse 44–45). Verse 49 adds that "the word of the Lord was being spread throughout all the region."

It was the same story in Iconium. There "a great multitude both of the Jews and of the Greeks believed" (Acts 14:1). Similarly, at Derbe, the apostles "preached the gospel to that city and made many disciples" (Acts 14:21). In fact, throughout the whole area of Iconium, Derbe, and Lystra, the churches "increased in number daily" (Acts 16:5). Surely this is what we ought to be crying to the Lord for—effectiveness in evangelism leading to daily increase in all the churches.

In Acts 17 we read of Paul's ministry, along with Silas, in Thessalonica. Here "a great multitude" of people became Christians. As a result, the opponents of the gospel had to admit that the apostolic message had "turned the world upside down" (verses 4, 6). The opposition became so intense that the apostles had to make a quick getaway from Thessalonica under cover of darkness. They went to Berea. They preached Christ to the Jews, and here, too, "many of them believed, and also not a few of the Greeks" (Acts 17:12). Once again, we are reminded that revival is not to be regarded as an insurance policy against suffering and persecution. Perhaps, in a mysterious way, the persecution of believers is part of God's wise strategy to further revival. We must not assume that revival will come without a cost. Costly effort in gospel work will be required. The possibility of the costly sacrifice of suffering is very real.

In chapter 18 Paul has reached Corinth. The story is still the same: "many of the Corinthians, hearing, believed and were baptized." (Acts 18:8). Even so, the Lord assures Paul that his full purpose of grace for this city has not yet been achieved. "Many" is just not enough for the far-reaching splendor of God's lavish mercy in Christ. So the Lord speaks to Paul in a vision and says, "for I am with you, and no one will attack you to hurt you; for I have many people in this city" (Acts 18:10). This second "many" is a vast advance on the first "many." The many still to come to Christ will make the many already saved seemed trivial by comparison! The "many" in verse 8 is plural, whereas in verse 10 the word is singular. Verse 8 speaks of many separate individuals, but the Lord looks forward to the emergence of a huge community of followers of Jesus Christ.

Acts 19 tells of Paul's work in Ephesus. This was the chief city of the province of Asia Minor. There are some striking statements in this chapter. Paul spent a few months over two years in Ephesus. By the end of that time, we are told, "all who dwelt in Asia heard the word of the Lord Jesus, both Jews and Greeks" (Acts 19:10). Later, Paul's opponents admitted "that not only at Ephesus, but throughout almost all Asia, this Paul has persuaded and turned away many people" (Acts 19:26). That is to say, the gospel had turned people away from idol worship. These statements can hardly mean that Paul personally preached to every person throughout the entire province. He spent those two and a quarter years in Ephesus. However, being the provincial capital, Ephesus was a place to which people from all over the province regularly traveled for business, or for social or cultural events. Presumably, people from all over Asia Minor heard the gospel in Ephesus, became Christians, and then returned home to spread the word to their own friends and neighbors. Here is a fruit of genuine revival. Ordinary Christians become quite open about what they believe. The gospel does not spread only because preachers are anointed with special power, but also because every believer becomes excited and enthusiastic about Jesus, and so the propagation of the word is multiplied many times over. Given that the word had traveled to every part of the province, we are not surprised to learn that Paul's activities "became known both to all Jews and Greeks dwelling in Ephesus; and fear fell on them all, and the name of the Lord Jesus was magnified" (Acts 19:17). Naturally, therefore, "the word of the Lord grew mightily and prevailed" (Acts 19:20).

Back to Jerusalem: the Impact Continues

By chapter 21, we are back at Jerusalem. James and the elders are now able to tell Paul "how many myriads of Jews there are who have believed" (Acts 21:20). A myriad is literally ten thousand. Given that there were already ten thousand believers in Jerusalem by Acts 4, there is no necessity to take this statement less than literally. Some people have modified the vastness of this number. This has been done in two ways.

It is sometimes read as the sum total of Jewish Christians from all over the world then present in Jerusalem for Pentecost, on the assumption that Paul achieved his stated aim "to be at Jerusalem, if possible, on the Day of Pentecost" (Acts 20:16). While the assumption is probably valid, there is no need to reduce the implied impact of the gospel in Jerusalem itself.

Other people speak of "allowable hyperbole,"[2] and see "myriads" as representing a large but undefined number. They find it hard to grasp that the number of believers in Jerusalem could literally have grown to thirty or forty thousand as a minimum in the space of 25 years. However, this again involves subjecting the word of God to our assessment based on present-day experience, instead of crying earnestly to the Lord to bring our present-day experience back into line with the infallible standard of his word.

2. Robertson, *Word Pictures*, on Acts 21:20.

The Impact at Rome

The book of Acts ends with Paul announcing to the Jews in Rome that "the salvation of God has been sent to the Gentiles, and they will hear it!" (Acts 28:28). If our mission is to the Gentile world, we have a wonderful promise here, which we must plead before God constantly in prayer. The Gentiles will hear the message. And yet today we struggle even to gain a hearing for the gospel, let alone to see people hearing and believing. If the Gentiles where we live are refusing to hear, then the truth of God's word is at stake. God has a vested interest in reviving his work, so that no one can ever complain that he did not do what his word said would happen.

THE KINGDOM OF GOD AND THE POWER OF THE SPIRIT

What was it that caused the word of God to make such a massive impact in those early decades? What is it that will have the same effects today? We can identify two answers to this pair of questions in the book of Acts. Both are found in the opening verses of the book. The first is mentioned in verse 3, which tells us that the theme of the teaching of the risen Lord to his disciples during the six weeks leading up to his return to heaven was "the things pertaining to the kingdom of God." The second is mentioned in verses 4–8, where Jesus "commanded them not to depart from Jerusalem, but to wait for the promise of the Father," which he equates with the baptism of the Spirit, and identifies as the source of power for worldwide Christian witness. We shall now consider the teaching of Acts on each in turn.

The Kingdom of God

The reference to the kingdom in the opening sentence of Acts serves to locate the book within the context of Jesus' teaching in the gospels, and emphasizes the point that in Jesus God's promised kingdom comes to earth. We have seen already how the Old Testament revealed the Father's appointment of his Son to be king, and we have noted that the kingdom is to be advanced throughout the world by the preaching of the gospel. Acts is the story of the start of that unstoppable advance. As Acts takes up the Old Testament predictions of the coming kingdom, and finds their fulfillment in the work of Christ, now ascended to glory, we are reminded that regular revivals, impeling the kingdom forward, are to be our realistic expectation for the entire duration of this gospel age.

The kingdom is explicitly mentioned several times in the apostles' preaching in Acts, and it is at least in the background in some of the reactions to the apostolic message. Moreover, some of the Old Testament quotations in the book are also rooted in this theme. As we saw in the gospels, Old Testament teaching is drawn into the New Testament and becomes part of the New Testament theology of revival. We shall look first at the additional references to the kingdom, and then survey the relevant Old Testament quotations.

Additional References to the Kingdom

Acts 14:22 summarizes the strengthening encouragement which Paul and Barnabas brought to the churches of Lystra and Iconium as they passed through on their return to Antioch. Part of their task was to remind the young believers that "we must through many tribulations enter the kingdom of God." Paul's preaching in Ephesus is summed up in these words: "he went into the synagogue and spoke boldly for three months, reasoning and persuading concerning the things of the kingdom of God" (Acts 19:8). When he later met with the Ephesian elders at Miletus, he described them as those "among whom I have gone preaching the kingdom of God" (Acts 20:25). These three references shed little extra light on the theme of the kingdom. However, there are a further three texts which give us greater insight into the content of the apostolic references to the kingdom. We read of Philip's ministry in Samaria that "he preached the things concerning the kingdom of God and the name of Jesus Christ" (Acts 8:12). We have already been told earlier in Acts 8 that Philip "preached Christ" (verse 5). Then there are two verses which mention the kingdom during Paul's time in Rome in Acts 28. Verse 23 tells of his witness to the Jewish leaders: "he explained and solemnly testified of the kingdom of God, persuading them concerning Jesus." Once the Jewish leaders had withdrawn, Paul "received all who came to him preaching the kingdom of God and teaching the things which concern the Lord Jesus Christ" (verse 31).

Both Philip and Paul spoke in the same breath of the kingdom and Jesus Christ. These twin themes are inseparable. The kingdom of God and the name of Jesus Christ are two sides of one coin. It is in Jesus Christ that God's kingdom comes. There is no kingdom independently of Jesus, and

Jesus is essentially and emphatically the king of this kingdom. So, if God's kingdom is to flourish and triumph, then we may, we must, expect the gospel of Jesus Christ to make unimpeded progress in every part of the world in every generation of history.

This reminds us of two vital things. First, revival does not come into a vacuum. It is as the church is busy about the work of gospel preaching that the Spirit is poured out. Second, the content of the church's gospel preaching is crucially important. God cannot bless error. That is to say, he will not bless fundamental error. It would be a bold person who claimed to have no errors whatsoever in his thinking and preaching. We are all prone to error, because as yet "we see in a mirror, dimly" (1 Corinthians 13:12). However, on the basic, essential truths of the faith we must be clear. It is only sound biblical preaching that God will use in revival. Christ is our message. And it is the biblical doctrine of Christ, his person and his work, his kingdom and his glory, which we must preach. Everything else which is included in our preaching must be subservient to this main theme.

Even the enemies of the gospel could perceive that the twin themes of the kingdom and Jesus had far-reaching implications for every other authority in this world. During Paul's time in Thessalonica, the unbelieving Jews complained that the apostles and their converts were "all acting contrary to the decrees of Caesar, saying there is another king—Jesus" (Acts 17:7). In a sense they were right. Of course, the apostles were not really advocating sedition, but it is true that Jesus is another king—the true king—and the advance of his kingdom must eventually lead to all the Caesars of the world bowing in recognition of his ultimate kingship, and submitting their rule to his. That applies to the governments of the nations, but also to those who hold authority in every sphere of life—education, the media, banking, industry, science, business, and so on. Our realistic hope is to see the steady advance of Christ's kingdom throughout the present age, to see every area of national life, cultural life, social life, family life, personal life, deliberately, intentionally, and gladly shaped by the word of Christ the true king. There is our New Testament mandate to pray fervently for revival.

Relevant Old Testament Quotations

We turn now to the relevant Old Testament quotations. The first such quotation comes towards the end of Peter's sermon on the Day of Pentecost.

PETER'S USE OF PSALM 110 ON THE DAY OF PENTECOST

Peter quotes the opening line of this Psalm: "The LORD said to my Lord, 'Sit at my right hand, till I make your enemies your footstool'" (Acts 2:34–35). As we noticed in connection with Jesus' comments on this Psalm (Matthew 22:41–46; Mark 12:35–37; Luke 20:41–44), it anticipates the total victory of his kingdom over all his enemies. A few verses previously Peter had referred to David's knowledge "that God had sworn with an oath to him that of the fruit of his body, according to the flesh, he would raise up the Christ to sit on his throne" (Acts 2:30).

THE REFERENCE TO PSALM 2 IN ACTS 4

The next quotation pertaining to the kingdom is found in Acts 4:25–26. Here the opening two verses of Psalm 2 are cited: "The kings of the earth took their stand, and the rulers were gathered together against the LORD and against his Christ." It is worth looking in detail at the context leading up to this text.

As Peter preached following the healing of the lame man, he said that "all the prophets, from Samuel and those who follow, as many as have spoken, have also foretold these days" (Acts 3:24). Although this text does not mention the kingdom as such, it is significant that Peter takes his point of departure from Samuel. It was Samuel who anointed David as king, and it is David's kingdom which was the shadow, the signpost pointing to the true kingdom to be fulfilled in Christ the Son of David. Peter's description of "these days" is focussed around the suffering and subsequent glorification of Jesus Christ. Those were the central events which inaugurated "these days." As a result of what Christ suffered and now enjoys, people may repent and find faith in his name, people may be converted and receive forgiveness for their sins (Acts 3:16, 19). "These days" are days of blessing (Acts 3:25–26), and the heart of the blessing is to be turned away from sin, in initial forgiveness and ongoing holiness of life.

But "these days" was not merely a description of the generation which had known Christ personally during his earthly life. In verse 25 Peter reaches further back into Old Testament history and quotes the promise to Abraham, "in your seed all the families of the earth shall be blessed." He goes on (verse 26) to say that this promise comes first to the Jews, implying that the extension to all families in the world will follow. So "these days" continue for as long as there are families anywhere in the world still untouched by the gospel. In fact "these days" is the entire period of history that starts with the life, death and resurrection of Jesus Christ, and continues throughout the gospel age until the Lord returns. This text highlights the Old Testament setting for the kingdom prophecies. The specific prediction of the coming king is part of the outworking of the foundational covenant with Abraham. That is why the New Testament opens with references to both David and Abraham in its very first sentence. The LORD once said to Abraham, "kings shall come from you" (Genesis 17:6). Whichever other kings were descended from Abraham, God's ultimate intention was the coming of Christ, the king of kings. The promise to Abraham emphasizes the massive scope of God's gracious purpose in Christ. If we know any family where there is as yet no one who is a Christian, then we have reason and motivation to pray for the continuing and expanding progress of the gospel.

And, as we have already seen, on this occasion the church did meet for prayer. The united prayer on that occasion began with an acknowledgment of God as Creator, a truth which implies his total ownership of the entire creation. To remind themselves of this fact boosted the church's confidence. Although they were facing the antagonism of the authorities, those who opposed the gospel were in reality illegitimate usurpers, failing to recognize the ultimate kingship of God. They then quoted the words from Psalm 2. They saw the rejection of Christ by the Jews and Gentiles in combination as the fulfillment of the Psalm's description of the opposition of the world's rulers to the LORD and his anointed. They then set the hostility which they themselves had received in the context of this climactic rejection of the Lord which took place in his crucifixion (Acts 4:27–29).

However, the use of Psalm 2 implies great hope. Those first believers would have been aware of the full context of the two verses which they cited. Here is yet another example of the New Testament drawing Old Testament Scripture into its own theology. This should not surprise us. As we have seen, Peter's words in Acts 3:24 emphasize the fulfillment in Christ of everything which the Old Testament promised. To read the Old Testament in the light of Christ is inevitably to find in its promises the rationale for praying for their fulfillment in the course of this gospel age. Where an Old Testament passage is explicitly quoted in the New Testament, it becomes obvious that it is a direct prophecy of Christ, and so feeds into New Testament theology. Our concern is the New Testament theology of revival. And

Psalm 2 is a key Old Testament passage which the New Testament takes up to stimulate our prayers for revival.

The first three verses of this Psalm describe the world's permanent hostility to God, which reached its peak in the condemnation of Christ on the cross. However, verse 4 immediately indicates that, to God, this resistance of his will and his ways is just a joke—as if puny humans really dream that they can throw off the sovereign Lordship of their Creator! They cannot, because, as verses 5–6 insist, the sovereign God has appointed his king, and nothing can frustrate his will in setting him in position.

Verse 7 is the turning point in the Psalm. The words "You are my Son, today I have begotten you" are cited in Acts 13:33 in connection with Jesus' resurrection. In Acts 3 Peter has viewed the resurrection from the perspective of God's reversal of human rebellion. Verse 15 especially makes this point: you "killed the Prince of life, whom God raised from the dead." We crucified Jesus, but God had the final word, and raised him from the dead. The rest of Psalm 2 depicts the total transformation which results from Jesus' resurrection. It does this by repeating several key words from the earlier verses, but placing them in a new light.

Four words in particular claim our attention.

"Nations"

This is the most notable of the four words. In verse 1 the nations are raging and plotting against the LORD and against Christ. But in verse 8 the nations are promised to Christ as his inheritance. This word speaks of a permanent possession received by right of succession. The Father is the ultimate possessor of all the peoples of the world. He is the universal Creator, so whether people recognize it or not, they do, as a matter of fact belong to him. In a sense, the Father has bequeathed the nations to his crucified and risen Son, and they will remain his possession throughout the gospel age.

The nations are brought into Christ's possession as more and more people from every nation are brought to saving faith in Christ through the preaching of the gospel, and the nations themselves are impacted by biblical truth, so that Christ is truly exercising authority by the word. That is what we mean by revival. In the early church's use of Psalm 2 there is an expectation that we shall see regular revivals until the entire world acknowledges the ultimate kingship of Jesus Christ. That is therefore our mandate to pray for revival. All we are really praying for is that the Father will fulfill this pledge to his Son, and bring the nations to him. If today things seem worlds away from such a state of affairs, then we must cry to the Lord to keep his word and honor his beloved Son.

"Kings"

Here is our second key word. In verse 2 the kings are leading the way in human antipathy to God. By verse 10 they are being invited to the wisdom that recognizes the ultimate king of verse 6, and that sees their own role not as power but as service. Perhaps we will know for sure that revival has come when the world's leaders openly acknowledge their accountability to Jesus Christ.

"Earth"

In verse 2 the earth is the sphere where human kings rule as God-haters, where they exercise their cruel power in foolish rivalry to God. In verse 8 the ends of the earth have become Christ's possession, so that by verse 10 earth's rulers have learned their true position as mere delegates of the true Lord of all.

"Wrath"

There is a significant difference in the uses of the word "wrath." In verse 5 the LORD addresses the world's leaders in his terrifying wrath. They reject Christ's authority, and all that results is that divine wrath terminates their rule. However, in verse 12 there is the possibility of taking refuge in Christ so that his wrath does not descend upon them. The word "lest" indicates a real danger, but also shows that the danger is avoidable. Here is the promise of a revival which will bring the whole world and its leaders into the blessed reality of the love of Christ.

In Acts 4:28 the church recognizes the sovereignty of God in the crucifixion of Christ. Even the world's rejection is subsumed within the overarching purpose of God. Even human rebellion contributes towards the goal of placing Christ at the head of all the nations. We need to remember this in difficult days. When the gospel is not progressing as we would expect, this is not because God has lost control. Even days of small things, days when Christians are persecuted, days of worldly defiance, are days determined by God's hand and purpose. Revival will not necessarily mean plain sailing for Christians. We may need to prepare ourselves for suffering just because there is revival.

As the church prayed, guided by Psalm 2, their concern was for the honor of the name of Christ. That is the import of verse 30. They were not concerned for their own comfort. There is a danger when we pray for revival that our motive may be the assumption that revival will result in Christians having an easier life. That is, in any case, not necessarily true, and, even if it were true, it is a very poor motive. We pray for revival only for Jesus' sake. We ought to be indignant for him if his reputation is not what he deserves, if he is not respected and glorified in the world, or in any part of the world, as he ought to be. His kingdom is the driving motive which impels us to pray for revival.

ACTS 8 AND THE THRUST OF OLD TESTAMENT PROPHECY

Although there is no specific Old Testament quotation in Acts 8, I think that Matthew Henry is correct to discern the thrust of Old Testament prophecy as a whole in the background to the description of the result of Philip's ministry in Samaria: "there was great joy in that city" (verse 8).

Joy is always a mark of the true believer. Whenever a sinner is converted he feels a joy such as he has never experienced before. When revival touches a town, a city, a region, or a nation, the joy is contagious, and great joy becomes the most apt description of the new social atmosphere.

Matthew Henry points out that "the spreading of the gospel in the world is often prophesied of in the Old Testament as the diffusing of joy among the nations." He cites Psalm 67:4 as an example: "Oh, let the nations be glad and sing for joy!"[3] Additionally we might mention Psalm 98:4, which issues this invitation to the whole world: "Shout joyfully to the LORD, all the earth; break forth in song, rejoice, and sing praises" (cf. Psalm 100:1–2). The prophetic vision was of the entire world filled with joy. And this joy is a hallmark of the kingdom. 1 Chronicles 16:31 says: "Let the heavens rejoice, and let the earth be glad; and let them say among the nations, 'The LORD reigns'" (cf. Psalms 96:11; 97:1). When and where the Lord reigns as king in Jesus Christ, joy abounds. In Philip's ministry at Samaria we catch a glimpse of the beginning of the fulfillment of that vision,

3. Henry, *New Testament*, Vol. 3, 139.

as people from the nations begin to flock to Christ. That in turn becomes a prophetic picture of the progress of the gospel until the day when the entire world is bursting with gladness in the kingdom brought by Jesus Christ.

PAUL'S QUOTATIONS FROM THE OLD TESTAMENT IN ACTS 13

Paul's preaching to the Jews at Pisidian Antioch, and its aftermath, recorded in Acts 13:16–47 is relevant to the theme of the kingdom. The apostle gives a whistle-stop survey of Israel's history. By verse 22 he reaches the point where God "raised up David to be their king," and in the next verse he says, "From this man's seed, according to the promise, God raised up for Israel a Savior—Jesus." A few verses later Paul quotes Psalm 2:7 as fulfilled in Jesus' resurrection, and then adds a further quotation from Isaiah 55:3: "I will give you the sure mercies of David" (Acts 13:34). Paul sees this as a promise from God the Father to his risen Son. It is a guarantee that Christ will never return to corruption. As Paul puts it in one of his letters, "Christ, having been raised from the dead, dies no more" (Romans 6:9). However, in the Isaiah context, these words are followed immediately by a statement of the extension of gospel grace to all the peoples of the world:

> Indeed I have given him as a witness to the people, a leader and commander for the people. Surely you shall call a nation you do not know, and nations who do not know you shall run to you, because of the Lord your God, and the Holy One of Israel; for he has glorified you (Isaiah 55:4–5).

The nations are to come running to Christ, eager to become part of his kingdom, because his Father has glorified him by raising him from the dead. He is destined to be the leader of all the peoples of this world. That is the promise of gospel success and the kingdom's advance in this present age.

As he finishes his address Paul urges the Jews not to despise the message of Christ. He does this by quoting Habakkuk 1:5 as a warning to his contemporaries:

> Behold, you despisers, marvel and perish! For I work a work in your days, a work which you will by no means believe, though one were to declare it to you (Acts 13:41).

Paul realizes the danger that the Jews might reject the gospel, because in Christ God has done such a remarkable and unexpected work that it is beyond them to believe it. The prophecy of Habakkuk begins with a message of judgment on God's people in a day of rebellion. The instrument of his judgment will be the Chaldeans, but the LORD will then bring judgment also on the Chaldeans themselves, because of their proud failure to recognize their subservient role in God's purposes.

However, in the middle of the passage dealing with the judgment of the Chaldeans, we find this amazing statement: "the earth will be filled with the knowledge of the glory of the LORD, as the waters cover the sea" (Habakkuk 2:14). Chaldean pride, or the pride of any nation for that matter, cannot continue indefinitely, because God's purpose is that eventually his own glory shall be known worldwide. Here the prophet looks ahead to the salvation of the nations in Christ. He anticipates the coming of Christ's kingdom through the advance of the gospel to the ends of the earth, leaving no nation, no city, no town, no village, no family, untouched. It is not just that the glory of the LORD shall fill the earth. That is already the case. That is always the case. That cannot but be the case, whether or not people recognize it. What is in view here is a day when that fact will be recognized, when no one will dispute it, when God's glory shall be not merely present, but known, throughout the world. Clearly, as the New Testament incorporates Old Testament prophecies into its own theology, it gives us an inescapable mandate to pray for such a revival as will bring these promises to complete fruition.

A week later Paul's fears proved well-founded, as the Jews of Pisidian Antioch turned against his message. However, the apostle then announced that he would "turn to the Gentiles" (Acts 13:46). He then quotes the second part of Isaiah 49:6: "I have set you as a light to the Gentiles, that you should be for salvation to the ends of the earth" (Acts 13:47). Here is another prophetic promise made by the Father to his Son. He is not to be the LORD's servant for Israel's benefit only—that would be "too small a thing," as the earlier part of Isaiah's text puts it. He is also to carry God's salvation to the very limits of the earth. Isaiah's next verse describes the impact of this worldwide extension of the gospel: "Kings shall see and arise, princes also shall worship, because of the LORD who is faithful, the Holy One of Israel; and he has chosen you" (Isaiah 49:7). Here is a vision of the leaders of the nations recognising that God has appointed Christ as the king of the world, and bowing to him in worship. The implication is that, when the kings acknowledge Christ as their true king, they lead their various peoples into glad and humble submission to the kingdom of God in him. Is this just an idle dream? Surely not. These are the promises of God, and, as Isaiah insists, he is faithful. Moreover, the Father is clearly concerned that his highly esteemed Son should get the acclaim which he is worth. We must hold on to the promises, and pray for the great worldwide revival which they obviously imply. We must be convinced that anything less is still "too small a thing" to do justice to the glory of Jesus Christ.

James's Use of Amos 9 in Acts 15

There is one more place where Acts quotes a relevant Old Testament passage. In Acts 15 we have the account of a conference at Jerusalem which convened to settle the question whether Gentile converts had to be circumcised and keep the Jewish food laws. The delegates recognized that to insist on this would compromise the truth of the grace of God. In his summing up speech, James pointed out that the calling of the Gentiles which they were now witnessing was a fulfillment of prophecy. He then quotes from Amos 9:11–12:

> After this I will return and will rebuild the tabernacle of David, which has fallen down; I will rebuild its ruins, and I will set it up; so that the rest of mankind may seek the Lord, even all the Gentiles who are called by my name, says the Lord who does all these things (Acts 15:16–17).

The LORD here promises to restore David's kingdom. But in so doing he has a great purpose in mind. It is so that all the Gentiles may seek him. The kingdom is restored in Christ. Its restoration is with a view to the entire world being called by his name. That is what we ought to expect during this present age. God has promised it. To pray for revival is simply to plead the promises of God.

The Power of the Spirit

The kingdom promises from God's word guarantee worldwide revival, but the power of the Spirit is vital to achieve it. Jesus promised his followers power for witness (Acts 1:8), and the testimony of a witness is designed to secure a conviction. By choosing this word, the Lord assures us that Christian witness to the ends of the earth will not be a failure—the world will be convicted and convinced of the truth of the gospel of the kingdom come in Jesus Christ. That power for witness comes through the baptism of the Holy Spirit (Acts 1:4–5). As we said when looking at the words of John the Baptist in the gospels, the initial baptism of the Holy Spirit took place at Pentecost.

We read about the Day of Pentecost in Acts 2. On that day "they were all filled with the Holy Spirit" (verse 4). That statement is true in two ways, indicated by the two previous verses. Verse 2 tells us that the rushing wind "filled the whole house," while verse 3 notes that the tongues of fire "sat upon each of them." The filling of the Spirit is an experience applicable both to the whole house and to each one. We need to be filled with the Holy Spirit individually, but also congregationally. We need both Spirit-filled believers, and Spirit-filled churches.

Some of the things that happened on the Day of Pentecost were unique and unrepeatable. The Day itself was unique at one level, in that it was the definitive fulfillment of the Old Testament prophecies of the outpouring of the Spirit. This precise phrase is drawn from verse 33, where Peter explains that the exalted Christ has "poured out this which you now see and hear." Other things that happened then might recur occasionally, but should not be regarded as normal. However, there are aspects of the Pentecost event which are general principles applicable for all time and in every place. There are some senses in which we should expect frequent repetitions of Pentecost, regular outpourings of the Spirit. As Albert Barnes has said, Pentecost stands as the model of a true revival, by which all subsequent claims to Spirit-empowered revival may be assessed.[4]

On a smaller scale, on a more localized scale, as in the home of Cornelius in Acts 10:44, outpourings of the Spirit will take place repeatedly as the Holy Spirit drives home the fruit of Christ's victory amongst the nations and people-groups of the entire world. It follows from this that we may confidently anticipate fresh outpourings of the Spirit whenever the gospel breaks new ground geographically or culturally throughout this gospel age, or whenever the gospel re-penetrates areas which once knew its power, but now need to be revived with gospel life. It follows that we should expect an ever-increasing sphere of gospel influence year-by-year, decade-by-decade, century-by-century, until at last all the promises made by the Father to his Son are fulfilled, and all the ends of the earth gladly bow the knee and submit to the universal rule of Jesus Christ.

4. Barnes, *Acts*, v.

And the Holy Spirit is the driving force in the expansion of the kingdom of Christ. This is his supreme task in the present age: to bring the nations to the Son of God, to save lost sinners in ever-increasing numbers, to spread the impact of the gospel message and the fruition of gospel blessing in every corner of the globe, to secure for Christ the crowning glory he deserves amongst all the peoples on earth.

Let us then turn our attention to Pentecost, and ask, which elements of the event are timeless principles? I think six things stand out.

The Spirit comes in Response to Prayer

Acts 2:1 tells us that the disciples "were all with one accord in one place." The phrase "with one accord" has already occurred in Acts 1:14. There we find that they were with one accord in prayer. We assume, therefore, that they are still with one accord for that same purpose of prayer as chapter 2 begins. To be "with one accord" is to share the same passion, and a passion is something that you are prepared to die for. I wonder whether our desperate need for an outpouring of the Spirit in this generation has become our passion yet? Are we devoting ourselves to prayer as they did? Those first Christians gathered in one place. There is something powerful about believers gathering together to pray. In those days the entire world Christian community could meet in one upper room. That is no longer possible. However, none of us dare neglect the meetings for prayer arranged in our own congregation. And united gatherings, bringing together in one place believers from various churches across a region are to be encouraged. God may well prompt us to meet in wider unity when he graciously purposes to pour out his Spirit again.

The Spirit comes at God's Sovereign Command

Verse 2 tells us that the sound came "from heaven," indicating that this was an act of God. It happened "suddenly," emphasising that the outpouring of the Spirit is not in our control. We cannot manipulate the powerful coming of the Spirit. No programs or gimmicks which we invent can bring revival. We may never think that as long as we have sound doctrine we are sure to be blessed. We are totally dependent on God. We are at his mercy. How wonderful to be sure, then, that he is a merciful God!

It could seem as if these first two things contradict each other. Surely prayer is something that we do. That is true, but we can only pray fervently for revival when God moves us to do so. It is not within our own power to stir ourselves up to pray sacrificially. Even our praying is a fruit of God's sovereign command.

The Spirit comes to Empower Communication

As the Holy Spirit fell on the company in that upper room, they "began to speak" (verse 4). Verse 5 notes that there was a multi-cultural crowd in Jerusalem that day, Jews and God-fearing Gentiles "from every nation under heaven." The outpouring of the Spirit resulted in the believers proclaiming "the wonderful works of God" (verse 11) "with other tongues" (verse 4). They were enabled to communicate in languages that the hearers could understand. To begin with the crowd simply heard a "sound," but suddenly, by the power of the Holy Spirit, the sound became "language" (verse 6). It is always like that. Preaching without the Spirit is just a sound. The gospel is unintelligible to the natural mind without the enlightenment of the Spirit. But when the Spirit falls upon the preaching, the gospel becomes meaningful language.

Our responsibility is to put the message across in the language of our hearers. In our contemporary generation, that can be hard work for those of us who have been brought up to know "the language of Zion" from our earliest days. We need the Holy Spirit to help us. But we need him also to empower the communication to the minds and hearts of our hearers. We therefore need constantly to pray for the Spirit to be at work.

The Spirit comes to Glorify Jesus Christ

That is what Jesus said the Spirit would do (John 16:14). On the Day of Pentecost we see it in action. After a brief explanation of what is happening (Acts 2:14–21), Peter simply preaches Christ. He tells his audience of Christ's human life as God's exhibition of power (verse 22). Then he moves on to speak of Christ's crucifixion as the apex of human rejection of God (verse 23), before declaring his resurrection as God's reversal of human rejection (verses 24–32). Finally, he proclaims Christ's enthronement and exaltation as universal Lord (verses 33–36).

The Spirit comes to Make Gospel Preaching Effective

Three thousand people were converted through that one sermon. That's effective preaching! Is that not what we need and long for? Then we must pray for the Spirit to be poured out upon us afresh. However, effective preaching is not just a matter of numbers. It also has to do with the impact of the message on the hearts and lives of those who are converted. They really are truly converted. They do not merely profess to believe or make a superficial decision. We see at least eight marks of genuine conversion in the experience of those who believed on the Day of Pentecost.

THEY WERE PROFOUNDLY CONVICTED OF SIN

Verse 37 says "they were cut to the heart." They felt as if they had been stabbed.

THEY SHOWED GENUINE REPENTANCE

In verse 38 Peter urged his hearers to "repent." They underwent a thorough-going change of mind and outlook and behavior. That is what repentance involves.

THEY TURNED TO JESUS CHRIST

Peter instructed them to "be baptized in the name of Jesus Christ" (verse 38), and the ensuing baptisms are mentioned in verse 41. Baptism signifies identification with all that Christ did for our salvation, and the commitment of our lives to obedience and service for him from now on.

THEY RECEIVED "THE REMISSION OF SINS"

Verse 38 again mentions this. They knew that they were made clean by the blood of Christ, clothed in his righteousness.

THEY RECEIVED THE POWER TO LIVE A NEW LIFE

Peter assured them that they could take "the gift of the Holy Spirit" now held out to them (verse 38). The indwelling Holy Spirit reproduces his own holiness in the lives of Christ's people. Unless that is happening, any claim to be converted is a sham.

THEY BROKE DECISIVELY WITH THE WORLD

In verse 40, Peter challenges his listeners to make a clear, clean break with the perverse world around them. That is invariably a result of real conversion. You cannot pretend to be a follower of Christ if you are still following the evil ways of the world.

THEY WERE FILLED WITH GREAT JOY

They "gladly received his word" (verse 41). They experienced a pleasure such as they had never known before. Joy is always a hallmark of true conversion.

THEY IDENTIFIED WITH THE COMPANY OF BELIEVERS

We learn this fact from verses 42–47. True conversion is not normally a merely individual thing. It results in participation in the body which Christ is bringing together from all nations. In exceptional circumstance this may be impossible. An isolated believer in a Muslim land, for example, may have no opportunity for fellowship. However, to reject fellowship when the opportunity is there is usually a sign that a profession of faith is not real.

We see, then, that effective gospel preaching is profoundly life-changing.

The Spirit comes to Extend Christ's Kingdom Worldwide

Three thousand people were saved that day, but in verse 39 Peter looks far beyond that one day. He says, "the promise is to you and to your children," embracing every subsequent generation. He continues, "and to all who are afar off," whether their remoteness is geographical or cultural. The Spirit will continuously extend Christ's kingdom worldwide for all time. Indeed, says the apostle, the promise of the Spirit extending Christ's kingdom reaches to "as many as the Lord our God will call."

There is one hymn which I would love to see torn out of our hymn-books. It was written by William Cowper. Actually, much of it is good, but verse 3 begins, "Dear Shepherd of thy chosen few." Where on earth did the idea come from that God's elect are few? Peter refers to those whom the Lord calls as "many." His choice of words assures us that the number of the saved will not be tiny. It is God's purpose to save very many—and our Reformed forefathers, such as Jonathan Edwards, Charles Hodge, B. B. Warfield, Lorraine Boettner, W. G. T. Shedd, and C. H. Spurgeon, believed that this meant the vast majority of human beings.[5]

Several years ago I read a striking statistic. It said that today there are more people alive than have died in the whole of human history until now. I recently heard that statement repeated. If it is true, and if there were to be global revival in this generation, it is easy to see how the vast majority of the human race could be saved. That is our sure and certain hope. That is what we long for. So obviously, prayer for revival has a definite New Testament mandate.

JOEL'S PROPHECY

We made reference earlier to Peter's explanation of the Pentecostal events. He stated that what had happened was the fulfillment of Joel 2:28–32, and quoted the prophet's words in full (Acts 2:17–21). As a result, once again Old Testament Scripture becomes part of the New Testament's theology of revival. We need to look at this passage and at Peter's inspired, and therefore definitive, explanation of its meaning.

The passage teaches that the mighty outpouring of the Spirit will make an impact on "all flesh"—that is to say, on people of every sort, specifically, on both male and female, on both old and young, and on people from every rank of society. Peter says that this will take place "in the last days." The use of the plural at least hints that there will be more than one mighty outpouring of the Spirit. In Scripture "the last days" refers to the age of the preaching of the gospel, the period of history inaugurated by the first coming of

---

5. See Marsden, *Edwards*, 505; Hodge, *Theology*, Vol. 1, 26; Warfield, "Predestination," 65; ibid., *Tertullian*, 263–64; Boettner, *Predestination*, 130–32; Shedd, "Larger Hope," 125–30; Spurgeon, "Heavenly Worship," 785.

Christ and concluded by his second coming. Throughout this period, we are to expect to see the Spirit being outpoured.

Joel 2:30–31 (quoted in Acts 2:19–20) is an interesting section because it speaks of things which are to happen "before the coming of the great and notable day of the LORD." In contrast to the phrase "last days," we have here a specific mention of one particular day. The day in question is the day of judgment, the day of Christ's second coming. Before that day signs and wonders will take place. They are spelt out in detail: "blood, fire, and vapor of smoke. The sun will be turned into darkness, and the moon into blood." Such descriptions are found several times in the Bible. Jesus used similar language when alerting his disciples to things that would happen "immediately after the tribulation of those days" (Matthew 24:29; cf. Mark 13:24–25), by which he means, as the context shows, the turmoil associated with the fall of Jerusalem in AD 70.

Such imagery is often read as an account of the upheavals associated with the Lord's return, but this seems to be a misreading. Peter clearly says that these things will happen before that day, and Jesus dates them after the tribulations which were to be experienced within a generation of his own time. In other words, they are the things that happen throughout this gospel age. Moreover, Peter prefaced his quotation of Joel's prophecy with the words, "this is what was spoken by the prophet Joel" (Acts 2:16). So the fulfillment of this imagery is found in the outpouring of the Spirit. We must remember that we are dealing here with picture language. Its significance is that the glory of Christ through the preaching of the gospel in the power of the Holy Spirit will eclipse all other splendor, even the greatest and brightest splendor known to us, that of the sun. In comparison with Christ, the sun will seem dark, and the moon will seem dull. It is the task of the Holy Spirit to ensure that that is the way things look to human minds and hearts. The Jewish commentator, Rashi, suggests that the sun will turn to darkness "to embarrass those who prostrate themselves to the sun."[6] This is a pertinent comment, and has a wider application. Any object of veneration, any ideology which is given life-shaping power, any human powers which are adulated, must fade away into total insignificance before the Spirit-empowered preaching of Christ in all his stupendous glory.

And what happens when the Holy Spirit does make the glory of Christ shine out as the all-surpassing splendor that it really is? Acts 2:21, citing Joel 2:32, tells us: people call on the name of the LORD, and are saved. Here

6. Rashi, *Complete Tanach*, on Joel 3:3 (Hebrew Text).

is one of those passages of Scripture which make the divine nature of Jesus Christ absolutely clear. The name "LORD" in Joel means Jehovah God. Peter quotes Joel, but a little later he declares that God has made the crucified Jesus Lord (Acts 2:36). Jesus is truly God, but the remarkable thing is that it is as the crucified one that he most clearly shines out with divine glory. That is because it is his death which has secured the kingdom over which he shall reign.

And in this gospel age, this era of the Spirit, this period of history when the glory of Christ eclipses all other splendor, the kingdom advances as people call on the name of the Lord Jesus, and find eternal salvation in him. The word "whoever" throws the door of salvation wide open—as wide as the world. It assures us again that the numbers of those touched by the glory of Christ, and saved by his crucifixion, will be vast. The final verse of Acts 2 reports daily additions to the church. This ought to be normal throughout the gospel epoch. So we should be expectant. We should anticipate fresh outpourings of the Spirit. We should pray for revival. We should plead the promise that the glory of Christ will be obvious to human hearts through the preaching of the gospel. If the situation is different today, then we have a far-reaching challenge to cry to the Lord for his mercy.

FURTHER OUTPOURINGS

There are some people who argue like this: the Holy Spirit was poured out once and for all at Pentecost, so we do not need to pray for any more outpourings of the Spirit. To do so, they might say, would suggest that we do not believe that Jesus has sent the Spirit. My reply would be as follows: if the Spirit was poured out once for all, why are we not seeing the gospel advancing with power in our land today? The outpouring of the Spirit is not merely some theoretical doctrine to which we can give our assent. We need the reality. There are two passages in Acts which demonstrate that there are some senses at least in which Pentecost is repeatable.

New Ground

We look first at what we may call the first Gentile Pentecost. Acts 10 tells of the first occasion when the gospel moved beyond the confines of the Jewish people. As this new sphere was opened up for the gospel, the Spirit was poured out in a way which resembled the events at Pentecost. Whenever the gospel is to break new ground, we must expect an outpouring of the Spirit. No progress can be made otherwise. We might add that we need an outpouring of the Spirit also if the gospel is to recapture lost ground. That is our situation today. We will not see the gospel advancing again, unless God intervenes powerfully by the Holy Spirit.

The story of Cornelius assures us that, when God purposes to save people from a particular community, he first prepares their hearts, so that there is a deep longing within them to hear the gospel. They may not know the content of the gospel yet, but they receive an awareness that the Christian message is what they need to hear. As in the case of Cornelius, they become conscious of the inadequacy of their present way of life, the incompleteness of their current worldview, and earnestly desire to know the truth in all its fullness.

Cornelius was a God-fearing man, who tried to please God through good works, and who participated in religious rituals (Acts 10:2). God's way of leading people to salvation in Christ may well start by bringing them to a consciousness of God, so that they recognize their need to adopt a lifestyle different from that of their contemporary environment, and different from their own previous practice. This God-consciousness is the preparation for an understanding of the fullness of the truth that God is known only in Christ. Cornelius was then impeled to send for Peter in order to hear the gospel (Acts 10:3–8). In the meantime God also prepared Peter for this approach from a Gentile (Acts 10:9–21).

On receiving Cornelius's message, Peter consented to go to Caesarea to meet him. Cornelius indicated his desire to know the truth (Acts 10:22–33). Peter preached Christ (Acts 10:34–43), and then "the Holy Spirit fell upon all those who heard the word" (Acts 10:44). The Jewish Christians were amazed "because the gift of the Holy Spirit had been poured out on the Gentiles also" (Acts 10:45). The wording of this statement closely echoes that of Acts 2:33: "being exalted to the right hand of God, and having received from the Father the promise of the Holy Spirit, he poured out this which you now see and hear." The Jewish believers recognized that what had just happened in the home of Cornelius in Caesarea was a repetition of what had happened to them in Jerusalem on the Day of Pentecost. Peter makes this abundantly clear when he later reports to the church at Jerusalem on this incident: "the Holy Spirit fell upon them, as upon us at the beginning." Peter then referred to the baptism of the Spirit, and pointed out that God had given the Gentiles "the same gift as he gave us" (Acts

11:15–17). Both events—Pentecost, and the outpouring in Caesarea were fulfillments of the promise that Jesus would baptize with the Holy Spirit. We conclude that regular Pentecosts are vital for the progress of the gospel amongst all the people-groups on earth.

Constant Need

However, it is not only as the gospel breaks new ground that fresh outpourings of the Spirit are necessary. Where the Spirit has recently been outpoured in power, the church should never settle back and assume that we now have all we need. Even in the midst of powerful gospel progress, repeated outpourings of the Spirit are needed. Otherwise revival will be short-lived. We see this from Acts 4.

In the context of the threats which they were facing the early church gathered for united prayer (verses 24–30). In response, the Lord once more poured out his Spirit. The first part of verse 31 says, "when they had prayed, the place where they were assembled together was shaken; and they were all filled with the Holy Spirit." This comment very much resembles the description of what took place on the Day of Pentecost (see Acts 2:4). This emphasizes the point that the outpouring of the Spirit at Pentecost was not a one-off event which could never be repeated. Rather, renewed outpourings of the Spirit are the church's constant need. As we suggested earlier, the events of Acts 3–4 probably took place within, at the most, a few weeks of Pentecost. Already God graciously pours out his Spirit again, so that the gospel impetus is not lost, as it would be, were such repeated outpourings not granted. This, surely, stresses that we must be constantly in prayer that God would continue to pour out his Spirit at regular intervals. The alternative can only be that the church will die out.

Two results of this second outpouring of the Spirit are highlighted.

Boldness

The first result was that "they spoke the word of God with boldness" (verse 31). This is part of what they had prayed for (verse 29). They did not wish to feel constrained by the opposition of their society, so that they stopped speaking up for Christ. When the gospel is despised, we can easily fear to speak, because of what the consequences might be. Boldness is invariably evident when the Spirit is poured out.

We too need to pray for boldness. Boldness is not something we can conjure up for ourselves. We are naturally timid, and therefore easily intimidated. Boldness is a supernatural gift. Only the Holy Spirit can make us truly bold for Christ. To be emboldened is actually part of what it is for the church to be revived. In conferring boldness the Holy Spirit secures the progress of the gospel of the Lord Jesus Christ. So from verse 33 we learn that "with great power the apostles gave witness to the resurrection of the Lord Jesus." The outpouring of the Spirit had powerful evangelistic effects. Such an outpouring is what we always need if we are to see similar progress in every generation. The object of our praying must be that God would pour out his Spirit once more, as we constantly preach Christ.

Love

The second result of the outpouring of the Spirit in Jerusalem on this occasion is described in verse 32:

> the multitude of those who believed were of one heart and one soul; neither did anyone say that any of the things he possessed was his own, but they had all things in common.

The rest of the chapter illustrates this fact. Its significance is that it speaks of a depth of Christian fellowship, unlike anything the world can know even in its greatest experiences of camaraderie. A revived church will always be marked by this intensity of love, this richness of mutual commitment and support.

A revived church is not just going to be one where the number of meetings is multiplied, but the members simply rub shoulders in a casual kind of way. When real revival makes its impact felt, there will be a new degree and quality about Christian love. The Ananias and Sapphira incident at the beginning of chapter 5 reminds us that, in such a setting you cannot play games with God. Reality is the only option. Holiness is the inescapable demand.

Acts 4:33 finishes with a telling comment: "great grace was upon them all." "Grace" speaks of God's kindness when it is totally underserved. It emphasizes that none of God's favors, nothing of God's goodness, come to us because of our merit. It reminds us that we deserve nothing from God, apart from his severe judgment upon our sin, and yet he has not treated us as our sins deserve.

It is important to remember this in connection with praying for revival. When God answers our cries and revives his work in the midst of the years, we can certainly not pat ourselves on the back and imagine that revival has come because we prayed so well, so fervently, so earnestly, in such large numbers, so sacrificially, or whatever. If God answers our prayers the only thing it shows us is that he is the God of grace. He has heard our cries in spite of what we are. He has come to our aid, even though we still deserve nothing of his help and goodness. And when the church is blessed with true revival the result can only be an overwhelming sense of how absolutely everything is the fruit of God's totally undeserved grace. Our very existence, our salvation, our service, our praying, our joy, our hope, our blessing—yes, absolutely everything is ours for no other reason than that God, in stupendous grace, has freely chosen to pour out his gifts upon us, absolutely in spite of the fact that, as sinners, we deserve nothing from him. Our response can only be gratitude and humility.

BUSY FOR THE GOSPEL

The picture we get of the early church in Acts is one of frenetic activity. They could not see fruit without the power of the Holy Spirit, but that did not mean that they sat back and left him to get on with it. They knew that it was their commission to carry the gospel to the ends of the earth in the power of the Spirit. God will not bless idleness. It is as we preach the gospel that the Holy Spirit will work. We must learn from the example of our first predecessors in Christ to devote ourselves to costly service for the sake of Christ's kingdom, for the love of lost sinners, and for the glory of God.

The busy life of the early church is highlighted in several places in Acts. Chapter 5 tells of another brush with the authorities in Jerusalem. As has so often been the case in the course of church history, revival and opposition came together. Again, we are challenged to remember that revival is not a sort of insurance policy against persecution. Suffering for Jesus' sake is an element in the Christian life even at times of immense blessing and advance. In Acts 5:17–26 we have what must be a top candidate for the funniest story in the Bible.

The Jewish leaders have the apostles arrested and put them in prison overnight. During the night an angel comes and releases the apostles. He instructs them to go to the temple and preach the gospel of Jesus Christ. So the apostles walk out of the prison into the darkness, and first thing the next morning, they start preaching in the temple, as directed by the angel. A little later the Jewish leaders assemble in council, ready to interrogate the apostles. Once they are ready they send a delegation of servants to the prison to bring the apostles to the court. The servants soon return with the information that the apostles were not there, even though they had found the gates properly locked and the armed guard in position. The members of the council are totally bemused at this report. But while they are trying to make sense of it someone bursts into their meeting with the news that the men who had been imprisoned are now standing in the temple teaching everyone. So off go the servants once again to collect the apostles and bring them to the court.

The council now starts to interrogate the apostles. The high priest wants to know why they have defied the order not to teach in Jesus' name. Even he has to concede that revival has broken out, when he says to the apostles, "you have filled Jerusalem with your doctrine" (Acts 5:28). In reply Peter insists that they have no option but to obey God (verse 29), and then takes the opportunity yet again to preach the gospel. Eventually the apostles receive a beating, the council once more commands them "that they should not speak in the name of Jesus" (verse 40), and then they are released. However, the apostles were undaunted. They did not lessen their gospel efforts: in obedience to God, "daily in the temple, and in every house, they did not cease teaching and preaching Jesus as the Christ" (verse 42).

Soon the gospel was to reach out beyond Jerusalem. Acts 8 begins with the comment that the believers were scattered as persecution mounted. However, verse 4 indicates that this was a tremendous opportunity for the gospel: "those who were scattered went everywhere preaching the word." In God's wise and mysterious providence, the suffering of his people was the means for yet further gospel expansion. And they did not fail to seize the opportunity. Acts 11:19–20 mentions some of the places where the gospel was now preached as a result of the persecution and scattering. This was the occasion when Philip brought the gospel to Samaria. When news of events there reached the apostles, Peter and John traveled to Samaria to strengthen the work there. When their task there was completed, it was time to go home, but they were not content simply to get back as fast as possible. Rather, they used the journey as an evangelistic opportunity: "they returned to Jerusalem, preaching the gospel in many villages of the Samaritans" (Acts 8:25).

The newly converted Saul of Tarsus showed the same gospel enthusiasm. After his Damascus Road experience, he stayed on with the believers in Damascus for a short time. Acts 9:20 comments, "immediately he preached the Christ in the synagogues, that he is the Son of God." When Saul later visited Jerusalem, Barnabas assured the church there that Saul had truly been converted, and told them "how he had preached boldly at Damascus in the name of Jesus" (Acts 9:27).

Paul continued to show this same boldness. When his life was in danger at Iconium he and Barnabas fled to Lycaonia, "and they were preaching the gospel there" (Acts 14:7). When he had the vision of the Macedonian man, Luke writes, "immediately we sought to go to Macedonia, concluding that the Lord had called us to preach the gospel to them" (Acts 16:10). There was no delay. There was a thoroughgoing commitment to get the gospel out to all parts of the Empire as quickly as possible. And the book of Acts ends with Paul in Rome, welcoming all who came to see him, and "preaching the kingdom of God and teaching the things which concern the Lord Jesus Christ with all confidence, no one forbidding him" (Acts 28:31).

And now it is for us to continue the story. We must preach everywhere, to all people, that Jesus Christ is king. We do so with the confidence that, in the power of the Spirit, through the preaching of the gospel, his kingdom does extend. We must not lose heart. We must pray for revival.

4

THE TEACHING ON REVIVAL IN THE NEW TESTAMENT LETTERS

ROMANS 11

Perhaps the single most important chapter on the subject of revival in the New Testament letters is Romans 11, especially verses 11–32. In this passage Paul maps out God's plan for the gospel age, and makes it clear that this plan includes mighty revival blessing. In the light of this teaching, the New Testament warrant to pray for revival is strongly reinforced.

In the first eight chapters of Romans Paul expounds the gospel and its implications for our lives as Christians now and our hope as Christians for the future. One word which keeps appearing in those chapters is the word "all." As Paul expounds the gospel message he is really thrilled with the thought that this message is for all the peoples of the world. He has come to see that with the coming of Christ something new has happened, and yet it is not entirely new. Throughout Old Testament times God's people were especially the Jewish people, but the Old Testament is full of promises of the extension of the grace of God to all the nations of the world. As the New Testament proclaims the work of Christ, it is describing the beginning of the fulfillment of all those Old Testament promises of hope for the world. So in that sense it is not new: it is simply the next stage of a plan which God had revealed from the very beginning. And yet it is new, in that it is now the fulfillment of what was just promise in the Old Testament.

As Paul comes to chapters 9–11, his concern is what happens to the Jews now. They were God's people throughout the Old Testament era. God's grace was focussed on them, not to be their exclusive right or possession, but so that they could be a channel of that grace to all the world. But when Jesus Christ came as the true Jew, the great Jew, the one towards whom the entire history of Israel was leading, his own kindred failed to see his significance. The vast majority of Paul's fellow Jews of that generation did not recognize that Jesus was the Christ, the Messiah. This causes Paul "great sorrow and continual grief" of heart (Romans 9:2), and so his "prayer to God for Israel is that they may be saved" (Romans 10:1).

Now, in chapter 11, Paul moves beyond his grief at the immediate situation, to ask this question: what of the Jews from now on? In the opening verses of the chapter Paul makes the point that it is obviously not the case that God has abandoned the Jews entirely. If he had, no Jews would have accepted Jesus as the Messiah. However, some did, Paul himself being an example (verses 1–5). So there is reason for great hope. However, at that time the number of Jewish Christians was just a handful in comparison with the number of Jews in the world. Generally speaking, the Jews had failed to recognize Christ. And looked at from God's perspective, it could seem that, generally speaking, he had rejected the Jewish people.

This raises the following question: "have they stumbled that they should fall?" Paul replies, "Certainly not! But through their fall, to provoke them to jealousy, salvation has come to the Gentiles" (Romans 11:11). At first sight Paul's words seem odd. He asks whether the Jews have fallen, and says "No." But then he says that through their fall something else has happened. He seems after all to be saying, "Yes, they have fallen"! But he is using the word "fall" in two different ways. The first use, in the question, means have they fallen fully, finally, and fatally, so that they can never have any prospect of return? Paul answers, certainly not that, but nevertheless it is a fact that his own generation has fallen. They have stumbled over Jesus Christ. They missed the fact that he was their Messiah, because he was not the kind of Messiah they were expecting. They were not expecting a Messiah who would be crucified. They could not anticipate that when God came in human form he would appear in weakness. So they fell in that sense. But Paul, inspired by the Holy Spirit, is absolutely convinced that this fall is not one that will just go on and on. They will not continue to descend further and further until they reach the point of no return. The Jews are not heading for the absolute end as far as God is concerned: "certainly not!"

The apostle then explains why that is true. The second half of verse 11 is the beginning of an explanation of God's strategy in history, and there are two aspects to it.

A "Revived" Gentile Church

The reason why God allowed the vast majority of the Jews of that generation to stumble at their Messiah, and therefore to miss out on the blessings of salvation, was so that salvation could come to the Gentiles, with the result that the Jews, looking at the Gentiles enjoying salvation, would become very jealous, and start thinking, "we could have been enjoying all that: why aren't we?" In verses 13–14, Paul says how thrilled he is that God appointed him the apostle to the Gentiles, because his work of bringing the gospel to the Gentiles is serving this purpose of provoking his own flesh and blood, the Jews, to jealousy, so that they begin to long for the salvation that Jesus has brought to the Gentiles.

This means that there certainly is a New Testament theology of revival. If the Jews are going to look at the Gentile Christian church and be jealous, that must tell us something about what the life of the Gentile Christian church ought to be like. But when we think of some aspects of Gentile church life, it is little wonder that the Jews have not been very jealous. That is why we need revival. That is why we should expect revival. And that is why we should not think of revival as something spectacular and unusual and occasional. Rather, it ought to be an accurate description of the life of the Gentile church at all times. If we are not revived people, if we are not living the life of the Spirit, if the love of the brethren is not obvious, if the exuberance of our praise is not noticeable, why should anybody be jealous of us? If we come to church and look bored stiff, if we are daydreaming as God's word is being proclaimed, if we barely open our mouths when we sing, if we never open our Bible from one Sunday to the next, then surely that is conveying the message to the Jews, or to anybody else for that matter, that there really is not very much in this Christianity thing. So why should anyone bother about it? But if the Jewish people are going to be jealous of the Gentile Christians, then God must intend the life of the church to be very different from that. Church life should be something phenomenal, attractive, stimulating, so that people looking on will think, "Wow! I want to be part of that!" If it is not like that, we ought desperately to be praying for revival.

A Phenomenal Revival

But notice something else here. So far we have skipped over verse 12. Let's now go back to it and link it with verse 15. In different words these two verses are saying the same thing. Verse 12 says that the Jews' fall and failure means riches for the Gentile world. But then there is an exclamation: "how much more their fullness!" And verse 15 makes the same point: the generation of Jews contemporary with the incarnation of Jesus Christ seem to have been cast away, but the result is that the Gentile world has been reconciled to God. But then there is a question: "what will their acceptance be but life from the dead?"

Paul there seems to be anticipating a revival even greater than the normal revived life of Gentile Christians that stimulates jealousy on the part of the Jews. At the moment the Jews have fallen, failed, been cast away. The result of that is that the world is enriched and reconciled. But supposing the Jews in their fullness were to come to Jesus. Supposing the Jews as a whole were to be accepted. What would it be like then? Well, in verse 12, Paul simply says, "how much more!" But in verse 15 he explains what he means: "life from the dead." In other words, if only the Jews as a whole would be provoked to jealousy and then come to Christ, recognising Jesus as their Messiah, then for the rest of the world the impact would be as great as the difference between death and life.

This helps us to understand some of the verses later on in the chapter. Verses 16–24 are a parable about an olive tree. The Jews as unbelievers are a branch that has been chopped off, but Gentiles have been grafted in. And Paul makes the point that, if God could graft Gentiles into the olive tree of his people and his purposes, then it would be easy for him to bring the Jews back in. After all, for centuries the Gentiles were outsiders, not as far as the promise was concerned, but as far as their experience was concerned, but they have been brought in. Whereas the Jews have been right there at the center of God's purposes for so many centuries: surely it will not be a problem for God to restore them.

And then verses 25–26 speak of a mystery, which is promptly spelt out:

> hardening in part has happened to Israel until the fullness of the
> Gentiles has come in. And so all Israel will be saved.

The phrase "hardening in part" is a description of the Israel of that generation and of Israel's history since then. It is a hardening which is only "in part," because there have always been a few Jewish believers, but neverthe-less, the bulk of Jews in the world have been, and still are, hardened against the gospel and against Jesus Christ. But here we read that this is only until something else happens, implying that there is a day coming when the hardening will be finished, and partial unbelief will be replaced by belief in full. And the "until" is when "the fullness of the Gentiles has come in." So we are now looking forward to a day when a set number of Gentile people have become Christians. And then "all Israel will be saved." The apostle now quotes Isaiah 59:20–21, which is yet to be fulfilled. It tells of the day when the deliverer, the Lord Jesus Christ, will come to the Jewish people as never before, and turn away the ungodliness which has rejected Christ. This is the fulfillment of God's covenant going right back to Abraham. God will take away the sins of the Jews.

The words of verse 26 raise two questions. The first is this: what is the meaning of the word "Israel"? There are some people who think that the word is not being used in this verse of the Jews, but of all God's people, whatever their ethnic background, that reconciled community, the church, comprising both Jews and Gentiles from all over the world and all through time. But that seems an unlikely meaning of the word here. For one reason Paul would simply be stating the obvious if that was the meaning. It is obvi-ous that everyone who belongs to Christ will be saved. Why would Paul bother saying it, if that is all he means? Furthermore, the word "Israel" has already appeared several times in chapters 9–11, distinguishing Israel from the Gentiles. So for the apostle suddenly to use the same word in a different way would be a very odd thing to do, especially when the reference to Israel in the immediately previous verse obviously means the Jews. So it is impos-sible to escape the fact that "all Israel" in verse 26 in this particular context has to mean all the Jews.

The other question is this: what does "all" mean? At first sight, it sounds as if the apostle is saying that there is a day coming when all the Jews without exception will recognize Jesus as their Messiah, will have their sins taken away, will be saved. But for some people that is such a remarkable statement that they find it impossible to believe. So they want to tone down the word "all." Perhaps it just means "a great many," but not quite literally "all." Now, I think it is true to say that the word "all" here is not back-dated. We are not to understand it to mean that the Jews of Paul's generation who rejected the Messiah will somehow be saved anyway. Nor is it talking about Jews who have been unbelievers in any other generation. But I think it is saying that all the Jews anywhere in the world who are alive at the particular time in the future that this context is speaking about will actually become Christians. That is part of God's plan. And if we find that too remarkable to believe, that probably says more about our faith than about God's ability!

That will definitely be a phenomenal revival, when every single Jew anywhere in the world is converted within the space of a few years—or perhaps not even that long! But now let's go back to verses 12–15. There seems to be an implication there that when this happens, there will be even more amazing blessing on the Gentile world. Otherwise what would Paul be talking about when he exclaims, "how much more"? Otherwise, what would "life from the dead" mean?

This suggests that when he speaks about "the fullness of the Gentiles" in verse 25, we should probably think of it as a sort of interim fullness. There is a set number of people whom God intends to save from the Gentile world by that time. Then "all Israel will be saved," but the impact of that on the Gentile world will be "life from the dead," another outburst of gospel blessing and expansion and power, with many more people being converted.

Clearly there is a New Testament theology of revival. And the message of this chapter is that, whatever God has done in the great revivals of the past or the present, it is nothing compared with what is to come. The revivals of history were remarkable works of the Holy Spirit, but the greatest revival the world has ever seen is yet to be. It will be a one-off. It will be at the end. There is a day coming when it will be obvious throughout the world—to Jews and Gentiles alike—that Christ is the real ruler of this world. And all the nations, Israel, and every Gentile nation without exception, will bow the knee to him and believe on him. "All Israel will be saved."

Now could it also be that all the Gentiles alive at that time will be saved, or is that again too big a thing to be believable? I'm not totally sure about this, but it seems that verses 30–32 do at least hold out that possibility, that when God does that final work of power in the world, he will save absolutely everybody who is alive at that time.

The point of these verses is that once the Jews disobeyed God, in the sense that they rejected Jesus, and therefore mercy came to the Gentiles through their disobedience, but God's plan is that through the mercy which the Gentiles have received, the Jews should again be opened up to that mercy. And then verse 32 says, "For God has committed all to disobedience, that he might have mercy on all." I think that is a better translation than inserting "them" before the first "all," as the New King James Version does. So are we to take this literally—that one day all the world, every single person, will receive God's mercy in Christ and be brought out of that disobedience into the joyful obedience of the gospel and the Christian life? I cannot be dogmatic about that, but it does seem to me that this is a possible reading of what Paul, inspired by the Holy Spirit, has written here. That would certainly be revival! And even if we stop short of taking the "all" absolutely literally, we still cannot avoid saying that it must be a spectacular number.

This chapter, then, is right at the heart of the New Testament theology of revival. It holds before us an exciting vision of what the church ought to be all the time, and what will be, as God's purposes come to their fruition at the end. This chapter therefore underlines the duty of praying for revival. That should take two main forms. The first is to pray that the life of the Gentile church may be revived wherever in the world Christians are found, so that the Jews may indeed be provoked to jealousy. The other is that we ought to pray much for the Jewish people, that God will remove the hardening, that he will open their eyes to see that Jesus is their real Messiah, that they will be converted and saved. There is no salvation for the Jews any other way than through the blood of the Lord Jesus Christ. They must come to him, as we must. We should be praying for that, for the Jews in Israel, the Jews in our own nation, the Jews around the world.

OTHER ROMANS PASSAGES

There are three other passages in Romans which are relevant to our theme. We shall glance at them more briefly.

Romans 4:13

Here it is sufficient to note that "Abraham and his seed" are defined as "the heir of the world." That the main reference of the seed of Abraham is to Jesus Christ is clear from Paul's words in Galatians 3:16: "to Abraham and his seed were the promises made. He does not say, 'and to seeds,' as of many, but as of one, 'and to your seed,' who is Christ." Here in Romans the apostle is alluding to the Father's promise to give all the nations to his Son. On the strength of that promise, Jesus Christ the Son is destined to receive the entire world as his inheritance.

Romans 5:18–20

These verses read as follows:

> as through one man's offense judgment came to all men, result-
> ing in condemnation, even so through one man's righteous act the
> free gift came to all men, resulting in justification of life. For as by
> one man's disobedience many were made sinners, so also by one
> man's obedience many will be made righteous. Moreover the law
> entered that the offense might abound. But where sin abounded,
> grace abounded much more.

I can still recall the thrill I felt the first time I read Charles Hodge's comment on these verses. Let me quote it for you:

> We have no right to put any limit on these general terms, except
> what the Bible itself places upon them . . . All the descendants of
> Adam, except Christ, are under condemnation; all the descendants
> of Adam, except those of whom it is expressly revealed that they
> cannot inherit the kingdom of God, are saved. This appears to be
> the clear meaning of the apostle, and therefore he does not hesitate
> to say that where sin abounded, grace has much more abounded,
> that the benefits of redemption far exceed the evils of the fall; that
> the number of the saved far exceeds the number of the lost.[1]

Hodge offers a truly great vision of the marvelous extent of God's grace in
Christ, of the vast extent of the Father's purposes for his Son. I have already
mentioned the statistic that there are more human beings alive in this generation than the sum total of human beings in all the previous generations
added together. The population explosion has been so huge in recent years
that worldwide revival now could easily result in the salvation of the vast
majority of human beings who have ever lived. That being so, we have every
incentive on the basis of this New Testament passage to pray for the constant revival of the work of the gospel in this world.

---

1. Hodge, *Theology*, Vol. 1, 26.

Romans 15:8–12

Paul quotes four Old Testament texts here, and the extent of God's mercy implied by these quotations gets larger each time.

The quotation in verse 9 is spoken by a Jewish person. The Jew says to the Lord, "I will confess to you among the Gentiles." Here the Gentile world is looking on as Israel praises her God. But then in verse 10, there is an invitation to the Gentiles not to remain as onlookers, but to join in, and to do so alongside God's people, Israel: "Rejoice, O Gentiles, with his people!" Then verse 11 is addressed to "all you Gentiles." All the Gentile peoples are called to "praise the Lord." Our thoughts are turned to one nation after another. Each nation is summoned to join their voices in a song of praise to the Lord, the worthy God of Israel. But this time there is no reference to doing so with Israel. The Gentile nations are now praising God for themselves. But in verse 12, we are no longer looking at the Gentile nations one by one. The reference is to "the Gentiles," all of them considered as a single entity. The "root of Jesse," the Lord Jesus Christ, "shall rise to reign over the Gentiles, in him the Gentiles shall hope"—all of them as a unit. The Gentile world as a whole shall be the kingdom of the Lord Jesus Christ.

We also need to look at the Old Testament contexts from which these quotations come. The quotation in verse 9 comes from 2 Samuel 22:50, a chapter which is reproduced in Psalm 18. It was evidently composed by David towards the end of his life, when he could look back and see how "the Lord had delivered him from the hand of all his enemies" (2 Samuel 22:1). David's experience was a precursor of the progress of the kingdom of his great descendant, Jesus Christ. This quotation anticipates the time when Jesus will be able to look back across the centuries of history, and see how his gracious Father, in faithfulness to his promise, has delivered him from all his enemies, and given him the complete victory, as he pledged.

The second quotation comes from Deuteronomy 32:43. It is the final verse of a song which the Lord gave Moses as a prediction of Israel's future rebellion and a warning of the judgment which they would consequently face. However, the song ends with a celebration of the Lord's faithfulness, even in the face of his people's rebellion. The last verse invited the Gentiles to rejoice with Israel because the Lord will provide atonement for his people. No doubt the apostle could discern the significance of this verse in connection with his theme in Romans 11 of the ultimate restoration of Israel. The atonement provided by Christ does in fact embrace Israel, and eventually they will come unanimously to recognize it and receive him as their Savior.

The next text is taken from Psalm 117:1. This Psalm looks forward to the united praise of all the nations, Gentiles along with Jews. It is a clear anticipation of the victory of the kingdom of God in Christ before the end of the present age.

The final text, Isaiah 11:10, is taken from a passage which anticipates with eager celebration the coming of Christ, anointed by the Spirit, delighting in the fear of the Lord, exercising righteous judgment on earth, and triumphing over all his enemies. Isaiah looks forward to a day when the impact of Christ's reign will be such that the entire universe will be restored to harmony, and "the earth shall be full of the knowledge of the Lord as the waters cover the sea" (verse 9). These words echo those of Habakkuk 2:14, to which we referred earlier. Once again we note that it is the knowledge of the Lord which is destined to fill the earth as completely as the sea is filled with water. Paul is quite clear that the Old Testament prophesies that Jesus Christ shall definitely one day be known and loved and worshipped and trusted and served from one end of the world to the other, that there will be no continent, no country, no city, no town, no village, no hamlet, no family, no person remaining outside his kingdom. And by quoting from this passage, the apostle draws the Old Testament hope into the New Testament theology of revival.

What is also striking about Paul's selection of Old Testament texts here is that there is one from each of the sections of the Old Testament as classified by the Jews. The Hebrews divided up their Scriptures into four parts. Genesis to Deuteronomy were known as The Law. Joshua, Judges, Samuel and Kings comprised the Former Prophets, while the Latter Prophets were the books of Isaiah, Jeremiah, Ezekiel, and Hosea to Malachi. Finally, section four was the Writings, and included Ruth, 1 Chronicles to Song of Solomon, Lamentations, and Daniel.

Paul quotes 2 Samuel 22:50, from the Former Prophets, Deuteronomy 32:43, from the Law, Psalm 117:1, from the Writings, and Isaiah 11:10, from the Latter Prophets. It is as if he is determined to emphasize that the entire Old Testament unites to proclaim this single theme—that the kingdom of Jesus Christ shall at last triumph in this world through the preaching of the gospel, with the ever-enlarging sphere of gospel blessing. Here again, it is blatantly obvious that the New Testament draws the teaching of the

Old Testament into its own theology, and therefore that the New Testament theology of revival is deeply rooted in the Old Testament, from which it can never be separated.

PAUL'S OTHER LETTERS

Here we look fairly briefly at five short passages.

1 Corinthians 15:22–27

This passage points up the great goal towards which history is moving. That is clear from verse 24, where we read "then comes the end." "The end" here is not just the finish, not just a full-stop. It speaks of the goal, the aim, the great thing to which everything is leading. In connection with that goal several things will take place, and the first thing mentioned here is the resurrection of the believing dead from every generation of history.

Verse 22 makes a parallel between Adam and Christ, but also a great contrast: "in Adam all die, even so in Christ all shall be made alive." If we read that verse in isolation, removed from its total biblical context, we might imagine that the apostle is teaching universal salvation, that absolutely everybody is going to be saved in the end. Some people have indeed read this verse like that. But that would not be consistent with the teaching of Scripture as a whole, so it cannot be what the verse means. In the next verse the phrase "in Christ all shall be made alive" is more specifically defined. Verse 23 speaks of "Christ the firstfruits, afterward those who are Christ's at his coming." The "all" in the phrase "in Christ all shall be made alive" is all "those who are Christ's." So in one sense there is a discontinuity between these two things. In Adam all without exception die: the entire human race, every single individual was plunged into death as a result of Adam's sin. But in Christ it is not as extensive as that. All who are in Christ will be made alive, but that is not every single person who died in Adam.

However, we must not read this verse in such a way that the two occurrences of "all" are so far apart in scope that the comparison breaks down altogether. As I have already indicated, I agree with people like Hodge, Boettner, Warfield, Shedd, Jonathan Edwards, and Spurgeon, who believed that God's elect vastly outnumber those who will finally be eternally lost. These Reformed predecessors believed that although the Bible does not teach absolutely universal salvation, nevertheless in the lavish mercy of

God the vast majority of the human race will in fact be saved in Christ, the vast majority will come to the Savior and receive his salvation.

W. G. T. Shedd gave a number of explanations of how that could be possible. Only one of his arguments is relevant to our present subject. He believed that there is a generation yet to be when the kingdom of Christ will advance so remarkably that almost everybody alive at that time will come to Christ in faith and repentance.[2] In other words he believed in revival, and he believed that the world has not yet seen the greatest revival that God has planned since time began. As we have mentioned, the result of the modern population explosion is that more than 50 percent of the people who have ever been born are alive today. So if, in our generation, there were a great revival that swept the entire world, then it is quite believable that the vast majority of human beings who have ever lived will be saved.

Then at the moment when Christ returns, the climax towards which history has been directed takes place. And the first thing which Paul mentions here in connection with it is the resurrection of those who have died in Christ. When he speaks in verse 22 of "all" being "made alive," he is looking forward to that great day. He is thinking of the resurrection of our physical bodies and our total restoration to real humanity which was lost in the fall. But as we know, that life is something which we enjoy in anticipation already. The life of the Holy Spirit within the believer is a foretaste of that resurrection glory.

The other thing which Paul mentions here that will take place at the end is that Jesus "delivers the kingdom to God the Father." He says that in verse 24, and then verse 27 takes up the idea. Theses verses are speaking of how God the Father has promised his Son that he will put all things under his feet. The apostle is thinking there of Psalm 8:6–8, where it says that God has put the whole of his creation under the feet of the human race. But Paul here, like the writer to the Hebrews (Hebrews 2:8–9), recognizes that this promise can only be fulfilled if we understand Christ to be the true man, the real human. It is in him, supremely, that the promise of Psalm 8 is fulfilled. Psalm 110 is in the background too. It speaks of the Father's promise to make all his enemies his Son's footstool.

So verse 24 speaks of this moment when the Father has subjected all his enemies to his Son and the Son hands the kingdom back to his Father. And verse 27 makes the point that when the Old Testament says that "all things are put under" the feet of Jesus Christ the Son of God, "it is evident"

2. Shedd, "Larger Hope," 129–30.

that God the Father who "put all things under him" is not himself included in the "all things." I think "evident" is a bit too tame a translation really. What Paul means is that it is blatantly obvious, it is a matter of basic logic that when it says "all things" will be under the feet of Christ, God the Father is not included.

We shall return to that in a moment, but first let's look in a little more detail at verse 24. Jesus is going to put "an end to all rule and all authority and power." Here "authority" and "power" are not two separate things, but one. We see that from the way that the word "all" is repeated: "all rule"—that is one thing, and "all authority and power"—that is a second thing. "All authority and power" is all the legitimate, legal, lawful authorities on earth which exercise their power, whether it is political power or military power, whether it is authoritarian power or power exercised in a more benign way, "all authority and power" will come to an end as Jesus becomes obviously the king of the whole world.

Then the phrase "all rule" is a very general one, and can include anything that has dominance over human life, anything that has a controlling influence. As Paul uses the phrase here the main thing he is thinking of is probably death. He goes on to speak about death a verse or two later. In Romans 5:14 he tells us that death reigns in this world as a result of sin. So the "rule" here, not necessarily exclusively, but primarily, is the rule of death in the world. And Jesus is going to put an end to that rule. That is what the resurrection is all about.

Verse 25 tells us that Jesus "must reign till he has put all enemies under his feet." The word "he" here must refer to God the Father. That is clear from the Psalms which are in the background. God the Father will put all enemies under the feet of Christ, but, until that happens, Christ must reign. This obviously means that the Lord Jesus is reigning now. He must reign until all his enemies are under his feet. Clearly that is not yet the case, so Jesus Christ is reigning as king in the world today. We may well feel like asking, why does Jesus not immediately conquer his enemies and bring them to nothing? Why does he not straightaway put an end to their rule and to all authority and power? Why does he not right now nullify their effectiveness and undermine their influence? But we cannot answer these questions. It is all in the purpose of God, and there may well be mystery along the way. Nevertheless, we do know this, that the goal is not in doubt: the believing dead will be raised from the dead, and the kingdom will be delivered back to God the Father.

Now verse 26 speaks of "the last enemy that will be destroyed." The enemies of Christ are many and various. They may include tyrannical governments that deliberately oppose the gospel and the church. They may include individual people in positions of influence, such as teachers who pollute the minds of the young with false teaching, or the entire education system which sets itself in opposition to the ways of God and puts itself in the position of being one of the enemies of Christ. But they are going to be destroyed. All the enemies who oppose Christ are going to be put under his feet. That speaks of total defeat. And of course, many more examples of Christ's enemies could be mentioned.

But "the last enemy that will be destroyed is death." The rule of death is the last thing to go. Along the way Jesus will be defeating one enemy after another. And this is where this statement is relevant to the theme of revival. In the light of this, we can anticipate a time when all those enemies who oppose the truth today will be brought to nothing and the world will be visibly under the feet of Christ, under his loving rule. Then all the governments of the world will be seeking to implement the laws of God. Their whole approach will be to ask, what must we do to serve the one whom we recognize to be our master? And no teacher will dare to say anything that is contrary to the word of God, and neither will they want to. And nobody in any position of influence will ever think again of opposing the truth, because Jesus Christ will be reigning obviously on earth. After that, finally, death will be destroyed when Jesus Christ comes again, and the resurrection, the goal of history, is fulfilled.

The implications of verse 26 are clear. If death is the last enemy to be destroyed, then all Christ's other enemies will be out of the way long before his return to raise the dead. There is our hope for revival. Here is New Testament support for this theme. The great goal towards which history is moving during the present era is a period when the reign of Christ will be a reality in this world, prior to his coming again and the ultimate goal of history as a whole, the resurrection of the dead and the restoration of the kingdom to the Father.

Therefore, we can certainly pray for revival. We must pray that the Father's promises to the Son will be fulfilled, that all rule and all authority and power on earth will be subjected to him. Because that is what revival is. Revival is not just some abstract notion that has nothing to do with Jesus Christ. Revival is Jesus Christ getting the honor and glory in the world that he deserves.

Ephesians 1:9–10

In verse 9 the apostle refers to God's "good pleasure which he purposed in himself." Verse 10 defines what that purpose is:

> that in the dispensation of the fullness of the times he might gather together in one all things in Christ, both which are in heaven and which are on earth—in him.

Here is a vision of total unity and harmony between all created things and between the creation and the Creator. As things stand at present we do not see such total harmony. The world is at odds with God, and consequently all kinds of disharmony tear the world apart. So-called natural disasters, earthquakes, typhoons, and the like, rip the natural environment to shreds. Friction caused by such things as violence and war divide the human race. The human race itself is out of step with the rest of creation, and so pollution damages the environment. But God's purpose is to bring this disruption to an end and bring into being a world at peace with itself because all people and all things are at peace with their maker.

Since this is to become reality in "the dispensation of the fullness of the times," our main task is to discover when that is. We get a clue from Galatians 4:4, which says, "when the fullness of the time had come, God sent forth his Son, born of a woman, born under the law." Christmas happened when "the fullness of the time had come." "The fullness of the time" began when Jesus was born of the woman, when he first came into the world. So when Paul speaks in Ephesians 1:10 of "the dispensation of the fullness of the times," I think he is referring to that same period of time which began with the coming of Christ into the world.

I say "I think so," because there is a difference between his wording in Ephesians as compared to Galatians. In Ephesians 1:10 he speaks of "the fullness of the times [plural]," whereas in Galatians 4:4 he says "the fullness of the time [singular]." So am I right to suppose that the two texts are speaking about the same thing, or does that difference between "the time" and "the times" suggest that the two verses are not talking about the same particular time in history?

Why do I think that Paul is talking about the same thing in two different ways? There are two different ways of considering time. You can look at the whole of time as a single entity: from creation to the end of history is the one sweep of time which God created. And the time reached its fullness, its climax, when Jesus was born in Bethlehem. That is how Paul is looking at time in Galatians 4:4. But in Ephesians 1:10, when he speaks of "the fullness of the times," I think he is looking at that same whole period of time from creation onwards, but thinking of it as a series of eras or epochs or times. Matthew does that at the beginning of his gospel when he divides the time from Abraham to Christ into three periods—Abraham to David, David to the exile, the exile to Christ (Matthew 1:17). And of course before Abraham there was another period of time. In fact we could perhaps say that there were two times then, the time from creation to the fall of Adam, and then from the fall to the call of Abraham. So you can divide time as a whole into this series of times. I think the distinction between "the time" of Galatians 4:4 and "the times" of Ephesians 1:10 is not between two different things, but between two different ways of looking at time as a whole.

If we look at time in its oneness, its completeness, all that is involved in time reaches its fulfillment in Jesus Christ. But if we think of time as a series of separate epochs, each with its own distinctive features, then every single one of them, each in its own distinctiveness, is focussed towards that time when Jesus comes, and the fullness of the times begins. This is the climax, the culmination, towards which the whole of time from creation onwards has been moving.

If that is so, it means that we are now living in "the fullness of the times." This is a biblical way of talking about the whole period between the two comings of Christ. Ephesians 1:10, then, is talking about now. This is God's purpose for now, to "gather together in one all things in Christ."

In other words, as we are thinking about the outpouring of God's Spirit, the reviving of his work, the extension of his kingdom, all these are simply various ways of speaking of the gathering together into one of all things in Christ. It is God's purpose to unite the human family first of all in Christ as their Savior, to bring into being a global church from every nation, and to do such a tremendous work amongst all nations that the nations themselves are brought into a harmony that has never been seen in history up till now. Peace will reign on earth. Wars will not happen any more when the nations are united in harmony. That is why both Isaiah and Micah foresee a day when the nations will melt down their weapons and remake them as agricultural implements (Isaiah 2:4; Micah 4:3).

And then, in a miraculous way, God will also unite everything else in heaven and earth in Christ. I rather think that when this great final revival takes place and the entire world feels the impact of the gospel and is united in Christ, things like earthquakes and typhoons and hurricanes, and anything which comes into the category of "disaster," will not happen any more, because God is going to unite the whole creation in him. God has a purpose in Christ, in this present age to unite the world in universal harmony. Here is New Testament warrant for believing in revival.

Philippians 2:9–11

These verses occur in the context of that wonderful passage about the incarnation of Christ Jesus, the Son of God, and his humbling lower even than the level of incarnation down to the depths of the cross. And then come the verses we are particularly interested in:

> Therefore God also has highly exalted him and given him the name which is above every name, that at the name of Jesus every knee should bow, of those in heaven, and of those on earth, and of those under the earth, and that every tongue should confess that Jesus Christ is Lord, to the glory of God the Father.

When does this happen? When will every knee bow at the name of Jesus and every tongue confess that he is indeed Lord? I have to admit that until relatively recently I used to assume that this was talking about what would happen when Jesus comes again, that on that day, when every eye sees him, no one will have any way of avoiding acknowledging that Jesus Christ is Lord. But I now wonder whether it is right to relegate this to the time of the second coming, or is this rather another promise for the time in which we live?

I think it could be, and for this reason. In verse 9 the verbs are in the past tense. God "has highly exalted" Jesus, God has "given him the name which is above every name." That is not a prophecy for the eternal future. That is something which God did in the resurrection. Ever since Jesus was raised from the dead he has had the name which is above every name. But why did God do that? Why did he give him such a name? Why did he exalt him so highly? The text gives us the answer: it is so that "at the name of Jesus every knee should bow, of those in heaven, and of those on earth, and of those under the earth, and that every tongue should confess that Jesus Christ is Lord, to the glory of God the Father."

Should we not be looking for and praying for a time before Jesus comes again when every knee will bow to him? Should we not be expecting a day when the name of Jesus proclaimed in the gospel will be so powerfully held forth that no one can mistake it? Jesus is Lord, and every knee must bow to him.

If I am right to read this verse like this, then here again we have a clear promise of God's revival intentions in this present age. And this ought to motivate us to pray with excitement and expectancy that we might see its fulfillment, even in our generation.

Colossians 1:18–20

We have now mentioned several times how many of our ancestors in the Reformed faith believed that God's elect were not a chosen few, but were the vast majority of the human race, and that those who would finally be lost were the few. One of the texts which they used to support this conclusion was Colossians 1:18, "that in all things he may have the pre-eminence." This is what Lorraine Boettner says:

> We believe that he who is infinitely merciful and benevolent and holy will elect the great majority to life. There is no good reason why he should be limited to only a few. We are told that Christ is to have the pre-eminence in all things, and we do not believe that the devil will be permitted to emerge victor even in numbers.[3]

It is not that Christ will have the pre-eminence in everything except the number of those who are saved, but that he will have the pre-eminence in all things. This leads to the conclusion that there is a day coming when there will be such a massive work of grace right across the world that the overwhelming majority of people alive at that time will become Christians, if not all of them. And given the population explosion, that means that the vast majority of people who have ever lived will be saved, and Christ will have the pre-eminence in the numbers as well as in every other way.

This is perhaps what the apostle is referring to in verse 20 when he speaks of God's pleasure "to reconcile all things to himself, by him, whether things on earth or things in heaven, having made peace through the blood of his cross." This text reminds us that the cross of Christ stands at the center of our expectation of revival. It is just because Christ, at the cross, made peace between a holy God and a fallen world that we may anticipate vast throngs of sinners entering joyfully into that peace through the working

3. Boettner, *Predestination*, 130.

of God's grace in the power of his Spirit. When we pray for revival, we are emphatically praying that the fruit of the cross may be reaped.

The vision presented to us in this verse is a very large one. It is the reconciliation to God of all things. Once again, the temptation is to postpone our expectation that this will ever be fulfilled to eternity. But maybe that is a misreading. Perhaps the apostle's vision is of the gradual expansion of gospel power throughout the world and throughout the centuries, until there comes a time in our present history when the vast majority of people are converted to Christ, and God miraculously intervenes to rid the world of those disasters and tragedies which destroy our peace today.

So in this text too, we have at least a hint that we are to expect, and to pray for, global revival. There is certainly a New Testament mandate for a concert of prayer for revival.

1 Thessalonians 1:4–5

Is it possible for us to know who God's elect are? It would save us a lot of bother in evangelism if we knew, so that we could just go to the elect. But we do not know, at least not in advance. That's why we offer Christ in the gospel freely to all people.

But Paul says here that we do know, with hindsight. He could tell these Thessalonians that he knew their election by God. This is not because he was an inspired apostle who had been given some special insight into the divine secrets. Verse 5 explains how he knew. Notice that it is linked to verse 4 by the word "for" (meaning "because"). Paul could know that these Thessalonians were God's elect because, as he puts it, "our gospel did not come to you in word only, but also in power, and in the Holy Spirit and in much assurance." When the gospel comes in power, there is no doubt that God's elect are there. Why would he bother otherwise outpouring his Spirit, bringing an assurance that makes the preacher so much bolder and more confident, and that makes the hearers so much more accepting and excited and thrilled by the truth? When God does that it is because his elect are there, and he is going to cast out the net and draw them in in great numbers.

Surely this verse gives us a very clear mandate for our prayers. As the gospel goes forth in our nation these days, we are not so conscious of the power. The Holy Spirit is not obviously at work. People are not filled with assurance at the message. Rather they make fun of it and dismiss it.

So surely we should be praying for something different—for the power of the Spirit and the assurance, so that it is obvious that God's elect are being gathered in, because they are coming in vast numbers in response to the preaching of the gospel. That would be revival. Is there a New Testament warrant for prayer for revival? There certainly is.

HEBREWS

The second verse of Hebrews 1 reminds us of the Father's appointment of his Son to be the "heir of all things." It is an appointment which took place before "he made the worlds" by the very same Son. I assume that we must understand the two clauses in the second half of the verse to be in chronological order. The very reason for creation was so that the Father could present his inheritance to his Son. God made everything as a gift for his beloved one.

There is no doubt an intentional echo here of Psalm 2:8: "Ask of me, and I will give you the nations for your inheritance, and the ends of the earth for your possession." However, while Hebrews 1:2 connects the Son's appointment with creation, in the Psalm it is linked with his resurrection from the dead, as a comparison of Psalm 2:7 with Acts 13:33 makes clear. Because of the entry of sin into the world, it was necessary for Jesus Christ to reclaim his inheritance at the price of his own life blood. By his resurrection he demonstrated that his death was effective, it had truly "purged our sins." As a result, Jesus secured the promise first given to him in eternity past. That is when he was appointed. Now he is free to ask the Father to fulfill his word.

Because his death was effective, Jesus "sat down at the right hand of the Majesty on high" (verse 3). There is a contrast here with the Old Testament priests. Hebrews 10:11–12 brings it out: "every priest stands ministering daily and offering repeatedly the same sacrifices, which can never take away sins. But this man, after he had offered one sacrifice for sins forever, sat down at the right hand of God." Old Testament priests stood, because they had to offer sacrifices repeatedly, just because those sacrifices could not purge sin totally. They never had any leisure to sit down. Jesus, however, offered only one sacrifice, because his sacrifice was perfect. As the cross loomed, Jesus said in prayer to his Father, "I have glorified you on the earth. I have finished the work which you have given me to do" (John 17:4). A little later, as the moment of death approached, he said from the cross, "It is finished!" (John 19:30). Now he was free to sit down.

After a busy day on your feet it is very pleasant to be able to sit down, to rest your weary legs, and to put your feet up. But Jesus does not sit down for evermore. Sitting at the Father's right hand is a bit like Jesus being in a waiting room. His name will soon be called, and then he will stand up again for his next activity. Hebrews 10:13 continues by suggesting just such a picture: "from that time waiting till his enemies are made his footstool." The writer there alludes to a Scripture which he has already quoted in Hebrews 1:13: "Sit at my right hand, till I make your enemies your footstool." These words are taken from Psalm 110:1.

The word "till" indicates that there is a time limit. Jesus will not sit indefinitely. The day will come when he stands up again. It will be the day of his complete victory over his enemies.

We remember Stephen. As he was challenging his Jewish audience about their rejection of the word of God, they became enraged against him, "but he, being full of the Holy Spirit, gazed into heaven and saw the glory of God, and Jesus standing at the right hand of God, and said, 'Look! I see the heavens opened and the Son of Man standing at the right hand of God!'" (Acts 7:55–56). It was a moment of victory, so Jesus stood up.

We may be thoroughly convinced that, wherever the gospel is preached in the power of the Holy Spirit, the victory of Christ is advancing. We may be totally confident that, whenever opponents of Christ become enraged against the gospel, the suffering of believers is a moment of stunning victory for Jesus.

Earlier on we read some significant information about Stephen. Like his diaconal colleagues, "he was a man of good reputation, full of the Holy Spirit and wisdom" (Acts 6:3). Of Stephen specifically we are told that he was "a man full of faith and the Holy Spirit" (Acts 6:5), "full of faith and power" (Acts 6:8). He was blessed with irresistible wisdom (verse 10) and an angelic countenance (verse 15). We may joyfully believe that, whenever Christians live lives so reputable that the only explanation is the fullness of the Spirit, Jesus' victory is being driven home. We may be utterly sure that, wherever believers live so close to Christ that the wisdom from above, along with a vibrant faith, a supernatural power, and a heavenly disposition are evident in their demeanor, there Jesus Christ is securing his ultimate victory.

In all such instances, Jesus stands up. This presents up with a great challenge. We have a part to play in furthering the triumph of our Lord. We must preach the gospel actively, constantly, praying always for the accompanying Holy Spirit power, which is indispensable if the gospel is to make an impact. We must be ready to suffer mockery and even martyrdom for Christ's sake, remembering always that our happiness and safety is a minor thing, that serving Christ's victory is the only thing that really matters. We must seek grace daily to live in a way that adequately reflects our allegiance to Christ, filled with the Spirit of holiness, who makes us holy people. We must walk closely with the Lord in daily devotion so that the presence of Jesus oozes out of us as we live the life of faith. Then Jesus must stand up again and again.

We must careful not to get the wrong picture here. We must not imagine Jesus spending the present era of time bobbing up and down incessantly: sometimes he sits; then there's a moment of victory, and up he jumps! I think Calvin is right here. He acknowledges that we find two different forms of speech in the New Testament. Jesus sits at the right hand of God. Jesus stands at the right hand of God. Calvin points out that both are metaphors and we should not take the language literally. But both metaphors signify the same thing, namely that all power belongs to Christ, that the kingdom has been given to him for ever.[4]

We can put it like this. The metaphor of sitting assures us that his atoning work is fully and finally done, that nothing more needs to be added to what he has achieved. The metaphor of standing assures us that his ultimate victory is in the process of being achieved through the work of the gospel in the world today, through the lives and sufferings of godly Christian believers. These two metaphors provide us with rich encouragement. Jesus sits at God's right hand—so the people for whom he died are conclusively, permanently saved. Jesus stands at God's right hand—so his victory over all the kingdoms of the world, his destiny to inherit all the nations without exception, is conclusively, unalterably guaranteed.

That ought to cheer us up no end! Today there seems to be such intransigent opposition to the name and honor of Christ in our land. Our government has legalized gay marriage, contrary to the principles of divine revelation. It is like shaking a fist in the face of God. Our schools brazenly undermine morality and truth. Strident atheism mocks the gospel. Elsewhere Christians face persecution from atheistic governments or from

4. Calvin, *Acts*, Vol. 1, 315.

Islamic extremists. But come what may, we know that what David prayed is the truth:

> Yours, O Lord, is the greatness, the power and the glory, the victory and the majesty; for all that is in heaven and in earth is yours; yours is the kingdom, O Lord, and you are exalted as head over all (1 Chronicles 29:11).

Jesus is standing up, because, whatever the peoples do or say, his victory is in the process of being secured. We may not always be able to see how history is moving towards the triumph of Christ, but we know that it is.

So Hebrews 1:3 tells us that Jesus sat down at his Father's right hand. Hebrews 1:13 tells us that he will sit at his Father's right hand until the Father makes all his enemies his footstool. The Father achieves that through pouring out his Spirit to create, empower, and enliven Christian life and witness. In between verses 3 and 13 there is a string of Old Testament quotations which serve to emphasize the certainty of Christ's victory. That is not their immediate purpose in the flow of the argument in Hebrews. The main point is the superiority of Christ to the angels. However, the texts seem to be selected deliberately to stress the fact that Christ is superior to the angels because he is destined to inherit all things, in line with the Father's appointment before creation.

Six Old Testament passages are cited. One of them (verse 7) focusses on the servant role of the angels. The other five focus on the glory of Jesus Christ the Son of God. These five are all taken from contexts which anticipate the final victory which is promised for Christ. Three of them are from contexts which we have already examined in some detail. We shall not repeat what we have already said, but just give a brief summary of their teaching.

The first quotation, in verse 5, comes from Psalm 2. This Psalm foresees the fulfillment of the Father's purpose to give his Son all the nations as his inheritance. The other quotation in this verse is the covenant promise which God made to David in 1 Chronicles 17:13. The Father has pledged that a descendant of David will occupy the throne forever. That promise is fulfilled in Jesus Christ, the king of kings and lord of lords. The text in verses 8–9 is Psalm 45:6–7, a prophecy which anticipates the steady progress of Jesus' kingdom, and its ultimate worldwide triumph.

The other two quotations are from passages on which we have not previously commented in detail. In verse 6 the writer cites Psalm 97:7. We did earlier mention the opening verse of this Psalm just in passing. It connects the world's joy with the LORD's reign. The Psalm returns to that connection in verse 8: "the daughters of Judah rejoice because of your judgments, O LORD." Verse 2 offers an explanation for this association: the LORD's throne is founded in righteousness and justice. So much present day human misery is caused by unrighteousness and injustice on the part of the world's governments. How much different it is where Jesus reigns as king! Verses 3 and 7 speak of the destruction of the enemies of God's reign. These are the people whose rebellion inflicts misery on their subjects. When Jesus' reign as king is finally secured, his enemies will be unable to stand. And verse 6 assures us that his kingdom will not be a small affair: "all the peoples see his glory," because, as verse 9 insists, the LORD is exalted high above all rival claimants to divine authority. The Psalm is portraying a timeless reality: the LORD does reign justly, his people rejoice, and the world cannot fail to see the marks of his glory. However, in the light of other Scriptures, there is a prophetic element to this Psalm, anticipating the full realization in history of the LORD's reign.

The final quotation (Hebrews 1:10–12) comes from Psalm 102:25–27. It looks beyond the present time to the eternal future. However, the preceding verses are full of expectancy that the LORD will work powerfully within the present time. The Psalmist writes at a time of trouble (verse 2). The source of the trouble is the reproach of enemies (verse 8), but the Psalmist accepts that this is something which the LORD has allowed in his indignation and wrath (verse 10). In verse 12 the Psalmist makes a staunch declaration of faith. He knows that there will never be a generation when the knowledge of the LORD will die out. So he cries out for mercy (verse 13). He is not concerned for personal relief, but for the LORD to renew his favor to Zion, to his people. He is convinced that enough is enough. The enemies of God have had their field day. Now it is time for the LORD to arise and exert his mercy in restoring his people's fortunes. His prayer is that the ungodly nations will come to fear the name of the LORD, that even the rulers of nations would respect the LORD's glory (verse 15). This will come about when the LORD reappears to his people in the glory of his grace (verse 16–17).

This context is remarkably relevant for our situation today. The enemies of the gospel are rampant. The church is at a low ebb. We make so little impact on our communities or our nation. We too must accept that this stems from the LORD's righteous anger. We have not faithfully represented him in the world. But all generations are to know the name of the LORD, so it must be right for us to cry out for mercy. There is a rising generation all around us living in abject ignorance of the most basic spiritual facts. But surely, enough is enough. We will not tolerate such things a day longer. We must plead with the LORD to come to us again in Holy Spirit power and restore the flagging fortunes of his modern day Zion, the church. But we do not want this just for our own comfort. We want to see the nations fearing the name of Christ, believing the gospel, so that his visible kingdom here on earth now becomes evidently glorious. A Psalm like this is a clear mandate to us to pray for revival. It may be found in the Old Testament, but its use in Hebrews draws its teaching into the theology of the New Testament, and challenges us to pray in our generation as the Psalmist did in his.

But the Psalmist's vision stretches beyond his own generation. He is concerned that the next generation should not be born into such a spiritually poverty-stricken climate, that works of gospel power would lead to the nations serving the Lord as part of his worldwide kingdom (verses 18–22). His vision is our hope. There will be a generation when the advance of the gospel has become so globally remarkable that all the nations, peoples, and kingdoms will be united under the banner of service for Jesus Christ. And that is the hope that sustains our commitment to pray for the outpouring of the Spirit, never giving up until we see the worldwide extension of the kingdom, and its establishment in every land as the dominating power on earth.

5

THE TEACHING ON REVIVAL
IN THE BOOK OF REVELATION

The last book of the Bible has been understood in several different ways. Given the diversity of opinion amongst evangelical believers about this book, there is no place for dogmatism concerning how we should understand it.

There are two issues. The first concerns the overall reading of the book. Is it a symbolic description of the period during which it was written at the end of the first century? Or is it an account of the final few years of history leading up to the return of Christ, with a brief glimpse at the end, of the world to come? Or is it a chronological account in pictures of the whole of church history? Or is it a series of symbols with no specific historical reference, representing the timeless battle for conquest of this world between the two kingdoms of Christ and of Satan?

The second issue concerns the millennium in chapter 20. Will a millennial age on earth be ushered in by the coming of Christ, as the premillennial views maintain? Or does a millennial period precede the Lord's return, as held by postmillennialism? Or is chapter 20 a picturesque way of portraying the entire gospel age between the two comings of Christ—the amillennial position?

On the overall reading of the book, I am assuming that Revelation is about the whole of the present age, that its relevance must not be relegated either to a past brief period at the time of the writer, nor to a future brief period around the return of the Lord. However, there are too many pitfalls in the chronological interpretation. There is so little agreement about what each symbol represents in church history. It seems much better to read it as a pictorial description of the spiritual battle constantly raging for the ultimate control of the world. So on this issue I am adopting the fourth position.

As for the millennium, I was brought up with premillennialism, but came to see weaknesses in that view. I have never found the amillennial view persuasive: it seems to me impossible to do exegetical justice to the book of Revelation as a whole on that basis. However, under the impact of the teaching of Jonathan Edwards, Charles Hodge, W. G. T. Shedd, Charles Haddon Spurgeon, B. B. Warfield, and Lorraine Boettner, to which I have referred several times already, I have been nudged towards the postmillennial position.

I now understand Revelation as an optimistic vision of the present age reaching its climax in the realization of the rule of Christ over all nations as a result of the Holy Spirit empowered impact of the gospel worldwide. This means that Revelation is very important for our exploration of the New Testament theology of revival. It is the Bible's final declaration of hope for the world in the preaching of the gospel, the summing up of the promises of worldwide revival.

I am convinced that the promises of God must outweigh contemporary appearances. We must read the current apostasy and unbelief in the western world in the light of the promises, and not read away the promises in the light of the state of the world. We may and must pray for worldwide revival because God purposes it, and our importunity will give him the signal that we mean business, that we are serious about it.

I do not offer this reading of Revelation in a dogmatic way. We proceed in a spirit of enquiry: is this a valid understanding? I invite you to assess.

REVELATION 1

The first chapter of Revelation serves two purposes.

Jesus Reigns

First, it sounds the keynote for the entire book. John's opening grace-wish reaches its climax in the description of Jesus Christ as "the ruler over the kings of the earth" (verse 5). Right at the outset we are assured that this present age belongs to him, and we are prepared for the revelation of his impending victory. This grace-wish is followed by a glory-affirmation, declaring that eternal dominion belongs to Christ. But this glory-affirmation includes a reference to Christ's people as kings (verse 6). Our role in the present age is to share in the dominion that belongs to Jesus Christ, and so to extend the influence of his kingdom into every corner of the globe, into every nook and cranny of human life.

In the Midst of His People

The second purpose of chapter 1 is to prepare the way for the letters to the seven churches in chapters 2 and 3. The final verse in the description of the vision of Christ which John saw homes in on the seven lampstands and the seven stars, identified respectively as the seven churches and "the angels of the churches." That latter phrase possibly means the church as God sees it perfected in Christ—a blazing star, as distinct from its earthly reality where we still struggle with sin and unbelief, and are at best just a flickering lamp. However, the uplifting truth is that the Lord is "in the midst of the seven lampstands": whatever the failures and weaknesses of the churches in their current earthly reality, we are not abandoned by our Savior!

The seven churches were real congregations in Asia Minor at the end of the first century, but they are representative of the whole church in every time and place, because the same issues keep cropping up in slightly different guise in every generation. Each letter is addressed to a particular church, but actually all the letters are for all the churches: towards the end of each one we read, "He who has an ear, let him hear what the Spirit says to the churches" (e.g., Revelation 2:7).

THE CHURCH'S FAILURES: REVIVAL NEEDED (REVELATION 2–3)

The letters to the seven churches illustrate why there are periods in church history when gospel progress goes into the doldrums or even into reverse. It is the sins and failures of the church which bring about such a state of affairs. The challenge to "repent" comes five times in these two chapters (Revelation 2:3, 16, 21–22; 3:3, 19). Prayer for revival must always be repentant prayer, in which we acknowledge our own responsibility for the dire straits in which we find ourselves.

When the Yorkshire ministers first issued the call to prayer for revival one of our concerns was our lack of real love for Christ as believers generally these days. That is why we are in such desperate need of revival. And that is precisely where Revelation begins in the letter to the church at Ephesus (Revelation 2:1–7). Here is a church to which the risen Lord says, "you have left your first love" (verse 4). This is the only criticism of this particular church, and yet it is serious enough to lead to the warning in verse 5: "repent and do the first works, or else I will come to you quickly and remove your lampstand from its place." The abandonment of love for Christ can result in the Lord's elimination of a congregation.

There is much praise for the church at Ephesus. They were hard-working for the Master; verses 2 and 3 refer to their "labor." They bravely endured through hardship; again verses 2 and 3 both speak of their "patience." They refused to tolerate sin (verses 2 and 6). They upheld sound doctrine and rejected error; they "tested" false claims to apostolic inspiration (verse 2). But without love for Jesus, none of these things is enough.

Part of what is involved in revival is that the Holy Spirit enables a church whose love for the Lord has grown cold to remember its first love, to repent of its lovelessness, and to repeat the works which gave expression to that first love (verse 5). Love for Jesus is the way to overcome, and so to enjoy real fellowship with Christ in a foretaste of paradise (verse 7).

One thing which the other three letters in chapter 2 have in common is allusions to the devil or Satan (verses 9, 10, 13, and 24). The letters to the churches at Smyrna (verses 8–11) and Pergamos (verses 12–17) refer to suffering, imprisonment, testing, tribulation, and, martyrdom (verses 10, 13). They remind us that the route to revival may well take us along the path of suffering as we face costly battle with Satan. Perhaps the honor and glory of Christ must be promoted by the persecution of his people. We need to be prepared for that, and to embrace it willingly as the cost of true discipleship.

I have said before, and I repeat it again: we must always beware of the danger that prayer for revival is motivated by our desire for a more comfortable life.

When the social and political tide runs in an anti-Christian direction, life for believers becomes more difficult. Until the last few years we have grown accustomed to a relatively easy life as Christians in this country. We knew what it was to be mocked on a personal level, but today we face a new situation. Some Christians are losing their jobs or ending up in court because of a Christian stance. Of course, these are familiar, everyday occurrences to many of our brothers and sisters in Christ around the world. If we are not careful, we can start to long for revival because we imagine that it will stop discrimination against believers. That is not a good enough reason for praying for revival. Our comfort must not eclipse the glory and honor of Christ as the primary motive. And if the route to revival is costly suffering for Christ's sake, are we ready to walk that pathway? Are we serious about being the followers of a Savior who was put to death? If we are not ready to die for his sake if need be, perhaps we ought not to pray for revival.

But when the devil cannot beat believers with persecution he uses another tactic. He sows the seeds of error in the church. This was happening at both Pergamos and Thyatira. The first of these two churches was experiencing Satan's attack and infiltration at the same time. In the letter to Thyatira references to suffering have disappeared. This is often the course that things take, making revival necessary. The devil first launches full-scale persecution against the church, but when that fails to destroy its life and witness he begins to insert error. Eventually, he gives up on persecution and concentrates on undermining the church from within. If we have fallen prey to this tactic, we desperately need to pray, repentantly, for revival.

In both these letters exactly the same words are used: these two churches "eat things sacrificed to idols" (verses 14 and 20). "To eat" is to have fellowship. These believers were compromising with the surrounding idolatry, probably to make their own life easier. A similar thing happens today whenever professing Christians compromise with secular idolatries such as the theory of evolution, or a pluralistic mindset which says that all views are acceptable as aspects of the truth.

But compromise with error inevitably leads to moral failure. Verses 14 and 20 both include also a reference to "sexual immorality" We see exactly the same pattern replicating itself today. Where Christians refuse to stand up against false teaching in schools and the media, it is not long before promiscuity, pornography, homosexuality, divorce and remarriage, start to get a foothold in the church. We must remember that false teaching is Satanic. That is the implication of the phrase "the depths of Satan" (verse 24). Compromise over such things as evolution or pluralism is not just an alternative opinion which merits consideration. It is devilish. And where it happens, the Lord becomes the church's opponent, as verse 16 and verses 22–23 show. That is why we need revival. If the route to revival is the pathway of suffering, it is also the highway of truth and holiness. And if we are not mercifully blessed with revival, the alternative is probably extinction.

But notice how Revelation 2 ends. Verse 27 quotes Psalm 2:9. We have referred to Psalm 2 several times. It is one of those Old Testament passages which are caught up by the apostles into the New Testament theology of revival. It assures us that all nations will, in time, bow the knee to Christ. Here the risen Lord passes on to his followers the very promise which his Father has given to him. Jesus invites us to share in his rule over the nations.

But what is it which breaks the nations and subjects them to Christ's rule? It is "a rod of iron." In Psalm 2:9 the word for "rod" is one which has two typical uses. It was used of a royal scepter of authority, as in Psalm 45:6, which prophesies the steady progress of Christ's kingdom until the day when it finally triumphs throughout the world. It was also used of a shepherd's rod, as in Ezekiel 20:37, where it is a picture of God's shepherd-like care for his people.

The word translated "rule" in Revelation 2:27 is also used elsewhere of a shepherd's care. One example is found later in this book. Revelation 7:17 reads, "the Lamb who is in the midst of the throne will shepherd them and lead them to living fountains of waters."[1] The verb "shepherd" translates the same Greek word. So the rod of iron is not some kind of metal crowbar with which Christ beats the living daylights out of the nations. It is the shepherd's rod with which he leads the nations to those fountains of living waters. It is the royal scepter which symbolizes his right to rule the entire world. It is "iron" because it is strong and sure and never fails.[2] It is the word of the gospel by which the nations' rebellion is subdued and the hearts of the people are brought to recognize the Lordship of Jesus Christ and to live under the scepter of his authority. When that finally happens on a world-wide scale, the ultimate revival will have taken place. And this text here in Revelation 2:27 reminds us of our role in preaching the gospel. Prayer for revival is never an alternative to doing the work of the gospel. It is as we do the work that the Lord will heed our prayers.

Revelation 3 is structured a bit like a sandwich. It contains three letters. The first and third describe dead churches. But sandwiched between them is a church, weak in itself, but bursting with the life of Christ. If we are like either the first or the third, we need to pray for revival, so that we

---

1. See also, e.g., Matt 2:6; Luke 17:7; John 21:6; Acts 20:28; 1 Pet 5:2.
2. Cf. Deut 33:25; Josh 17:18; Dan 2:40, 42; 7:7.

become more like the wholesome filling in this sandwich. Let's look at the two outer letters first, and then come to the middle one.

The church at Sardis had a fine reputation. How devastating, then, for them to hear the risen Lord announce his assessment: "you have a name that you are alive, and yet you are dead" (Revelation 3:1). When a church is dead, it desperately needs revival.

We are not told exactly what the problem at Sardis was, but there is perhaps a clue in the opening phrase of verse 3: "remember therefore how you have received and heard." The twin concepts, receiving and hearing, sum up biblical faith. In 1 Corinthians 4:7 the apostle contrasts receiving and boasting. They are two fundamentally opposed attitudes to life. The uniqueness of biblical faith is that we hear the gospel word, and we receive what God gives us in Christ. All other religions, all secular views, are driven by the basic instinct of the sinful human heart—do your best, make your own way in the world, earn your salvation. That is the expression of sinful human boasting.

Was the problem at Sardis that the church had drifted away from the attitude of a receiver into sinful boasting? It had a fine reputation, but pervading its life there was a spirit of pride such that the believers there had forgotten their position as receivers.

It is so easy to slip like that from a joyful receiving of the gospel message into a boastful attitude of self-righteousness, so easy to begin with the knowledge that my good works count for nothing, that Christ alone must save me, and then to lapse into a Christian life that assumes that I must impress God by my spiritual devotion. It is so easy for an evangelical church to become inflated with pride at its own soundness, at its busy evangelistic program, at the numbers attending the prayer meeting, and the Lord replies, "you are dead."

So what is the solution? The key is a verb which the Lord uses twice in verses 2 and 3. It is translated slightly differently each time by the New King James Version. Verse 2 says "be watchful," and verse 3 uses the single word "watch." The idea is "wake up!" When a church is sleeping the sleep of death, it needs to be woken up. As the hymn puts it,

> Revive thy work, O Lord,
> Thy mighty arm make bare;
> Speak with the voice that wakes the dead,
> And make thy people hear.

Revive thy work, O Lord,
Disturb this sleep of death;
Quicken the smoldering embers now
By thine almighty breath.[3]

Evidently there were some "smoldering embers" at Sardis. Verse 2 speaks of "the things which remain, that are ready to die," while verse 4 acknowledges that "you have a few names even in Sardis who have not defiled their garments." The boasting attitude has not yet corrupted the entire organization. But when the defiling power of boasting starts to get a hold on a congregation, the only hope is that the Holy Spirit will cause the gospel of God's grace to strike home afresh so powerfully that the church wakes up again to the fact that all we ever are before God is receivers, that he alone is the almighty, infinite, benevolent giver, that we are nothing, that we contribute nothing, but that Jesus paid it all, that Christ alone is all in all to us. That is the revival which we need.

The deadness of the church at Laodicea is portrayed in terms of lukewarmness (Revelation 3:15–16). On a hot summer's day, there are two things that can refresh you. One is a piping hot cup of tea. The other is an icy cold glass of water. What you definitely do not want is an eighty degree cup of tea from a pot which was brewed several minutes after the kettle had gone off the boil. Nor do you want a glass of water that has been standing around in the blazing sun for half an hour and is now rather horribly tepid. Neither of those lukewarm drinks serves any useful purpose. All you want to do is rapidly spit them out of your mouth. And that is the problem with a Laodicean type of church: it serves no useful purpose. And all that God wants to do is spew them out (verse 16).

The problem at Laodicea was that the church members had an exaggerated view of what they had already received. They had become content with a very lackluster spiritual life. They thought that they were rich and wealthy, that they had everything they needed, whereas in reality they were "wretched, miserable, poor, blind, and naked" (verse 17).

This is an easy trap for an evangelical church to fall into. Because we are biblically sound and evangelistically active, because we are great at mutual support in times of need, we start to think, "we've got it all, we're just fine," and yet the danger is that all our church life becomes merely external. We are missing the depth of relationship with Christ depicted in the image of dining with him in verse 20. Consequently, despite all our activities,

3. By Albert Midlane, 1825–1909.

all our soundness, despite the commitment of the members, we are really powerless and ineffective. Spiritual vibrancy and vitality are lacking.

Such a church needs to open the door to Christ all over again. As verse 18 implies, it needs to go shopping from the abundance of the Lord's gracious provision. It needs to be revived by the renewed intimacy of his living presence.

When the risen Christ introduces himself to the church at Philadelphia in Revelation 3:7, he takes up the reference to keys in 1:18, and amplifies it by quoting Isaiah 22:22 in order to apply the prophecy to himself: "These things says he who is holy, he who is true, he who has the key of David, he who opens and no one shuts, and shuts and no one opens." Isaiah used those words of one Eliakim, who turned out to be a disappointment. Jesus is the true fulfillment, and there is no disappointment in him. He holds the royal key to the house of David. He has the authority over all things. Verse 8 then explains the significance of the keys for the church: "I have set before you an open door, and no one can shut it." Even a church which seems to have "little strength" (verse 8) may press through the door with the delegated authority of Christ, and be used to extend his kingdom.

The tragedy of churches like Sardis or Laodicea is that they cannot press through the open door, because dead bodies cannot go anywhere. We must pray for revival: we need to rise from our deadness and win the world for Christ in the power of his Holy Spirit.

PRAYER AND PROCLAMATION: OUR SHARE IN REVIVAL (REVELATION 4–5)

In Revelation 4:1 we are invited to "come up" to heaven. We see God there on his throne. "Around the throne" we see twenty-four elders (verse 4), symbolic of God's people throughout the generations, and "in the midst of the throne" there are four living creatures—one wild, one domestic, one human, and one flying (verse 6)—representing the entire creation. Both groups inhabit the earth, for the important thing is that the earth is the focus of God's rule. In fact, God's rule is the central fact about life on earth. It is a striking statement that the four living creatures are "in the midst of the throne." God's throne is the greater reality. Creation is in the middle of it, and not the other way round. God's rule is not limited to a central point in creation. Its influence extends absolutely everywhere.

As we come to the beginning of chapter 5 our attention is drawn to the sealed scroll held in God's hand. This scroll is the textbook of history, the record of God's plan and purpose. It is the proclamation of the goal of history and the route by which the goal will be reached.

However, up until Revelation 5:2 this passage has merely been setting the scene. At this point a job advertisement is published: "Who is worthy to open the scroll and to loose its seals?" (Revelation 5:2). God wants to exercise his rule over the earth via a delegated intermediary.

In verse 3 some potential candidates for the job are considered. They come in three categories. Heavenly beings, earthly beings, and subterranean beings are all considered, and all alike disqualified. The frustration of God's desire drives John to tears (verse 4).

But suddenly a new candidate, the ideal candidate, appears! The announcement is made in verse 5. The one qualified candidate for the job of ruling the earth on God's behalf is Jesus Christ, and this chapter is a symbolic description of his ascension. After his life on earth he is lifted up to heaven to fill the vacancy that only he can fill.

Initially Jesus is portrayed as "the lion of the tribe of Judah." In the background are the words of Genesis 49:9–10:

> Judah is a lion's whelp; from the prey, my son, you have gone up.
> He bows down, he lies down as a lion; and as a lion, who shall
> rouse him? The scepter shall not depart from Judah, nor a lawgiver
> from between his feet, until Shiloh comes; and to him shall be the
> obedience of the people.

Judah is here described both as a lion, and as the possessor of the scepter, the symbol of rule and authority. In Jesus Christ this prophecy is fulfilled. The announcement in Revelation 5:2 also indicates the chief qualification required for this job of delegated ruler on God's behalf. The quality which Jesus had, in which all the other candidates were conspicuously lacking, was that he "has prevailed." He won a decisive victory. He defeated Satan. We are reminded of the words of 1 John 3:8: "For this purpose the Son of God was manifested, that he might destroy the works of the devil." And in that purpose he was a success. That is the clinching fact which qualifies him for ruling the earth.

But when John looks to see the lion, what in fact greets his vision is "a lamb as though it has been slain." Here we find the secret of his victory. Now we are reminded of Colossians 2:15, which tells us that Jesus Christ "disarmed principalities and powers," and "made a public spectacle of them, triumphing over them in it" (the cross). The lamb slain is the language of sacrifice. By the sacrifice which atoned for his people's sins, Jesus also defeated Satan. He broke Satan's hold over the world, because it is sin which is the bond between the devil and the human race.

The end of chapter 5 depicts heaven's glad relief. There is a suitable candidate for this vacant post. The position is filled. God's rule over the earth will be administered. God's purposes shall not stall.

This passage contains three notes which emphasize our part in the worldwide progress of the gospel. The first two we can take together. Revelation 4:4 has the elders sitting on thrones around the throne. This is symbolic of the church's share in the reign of Christ. Revelation 5:10 makes the same point when it describes us as "kings and priests to our God," and declares that "we shall reign on the earth." We wield the rod of the gospel. In our evangelism, in all our efforts to uphold Christ's authority in politics, in the school, in the workplace, in the home, whenever we stand up for the truth in a world which rebelliously defies God's law, we share as kings in the reign of Jesus.

The third verse which we note is Revelation 5:8, which speaks of "the prayers of the saints." The bowls of incense which symbolize the church's prayers are held by the four living creatures as well as by the twenty-four elders. That is a way of saying that the effects of our prayers permeate the whole creation. When we pray, we are not wasting our time. Prayer is not a meaningless ritual. The whole creation is impacted by the effects of the prayers of God's people. We have a phenomenal part to play in the progress of the kingdom of Jesus towards its ultimate victory.

Our role, then, is twofold: we pray, and we are active in gospel proclamation and gospel application. Activism without prayer will never be effective. Prayer without action is equally useless. Prayer hand-in-hand with energetic service—that is how God invites us to share in the work of revival, of bringing the whole world to Christ.

JESUS CONQUERS: REVIVAL EXPECTED (REVELATION 6–7)

As chapter 6 begins, Jesus Christ starts opening the seals to disclose the contents of the scroll. The first thing which we see is a symbol of Jesus Christ riding forth to conquer the world (verse 2).[4] That comes first be-

4. There are differences of opinion amongst Bible scholars on the interpretation

cause it is the thing of paramount importance. In the chapters that follow we hear a lot about wars, disasters, persecutions, we observe the devil at work in human history. But the starting point is not the devil's activity. The starting point is Jesus conquering. Whatever else we might say about the history of the world since the ascension of Christ to heaven, the one vital thing is that he is conquering the nations by the rod of the gospel. That is the defining truth of the age in which we live. Everything is moving in his direction. We are to expect the full achievement of that conquest, the triumph of his kingdom in the world, the victory of the gospel, as the nations are subdued to Christ's gracious rule.

We should, therefore, be expecting to see the gospel achieving victory after victory throughout the present age. A gospel victory may take the form both of an individual conversion and of a regional transformation. So we ought to anticipate both regular conversions and repeated revivals. We need to raise ourselves out of our hopelessness (or rather to ask the Holy Spirit to revive us from our despondency). We need confidently to believe that no gospel effort will fail to achieve its purpose, that sinners must be saved constantly, that revivals will occur regularly, until the world is finally and fully conquered by Christ.

What follows is not intended to undermine that confidence. The following verses illustrate the permanent features of life in a sinful world, especially during the period since Christ's ascension to heaven. The second seal is a picture of war (Revelation 6:4). The third seal depicts economic crisis (Revelation 6:6), and the fourth seal portrays death as a result of violence, famine, disease, and natural disasters in general (Revelation 6:8). All these experiences are the kinds of things which we can expect to see happening in the present age. The fifth seal includes the persecution of God's people as a permanent feature of life in the present world (Revelation 6:9–10).

The message of the sixth seal is that in a world such as that described by the first five seals, the gospel still goes forth, and makes its massive impact on all nations. Revelation 6:12–14 uses the familiar biblical imagery of the sun being darkened. We saw earlier that this is a poetic description of the brightness of Christ, which eclipses all other glory. As the gospel is preached, it is the task of the Holy Spirit to radiate to the world the dazzling splendor of Jesus. Verses 15–17 emphasize the normal reaction of sinful

---

of some of the details of Revelation's symbolism. This book is not the place to discuss different views in detail. I shall simply say what my conclusion is as to the meaning of the symbols. Those who are interested in the alternative views must consult the larger commentaries.

human beings to the glory of Christ: there is a deep-seated awareness that we must hide from God. Those who refuse the grace of the gospel have no option but to encounter its wrath.

However, rejection of the gospel is not the major thing. Chapter 7 illustrates the security of God's people, even in a world of violence, disaster, and persecution. The first part of the chapter proclaims hope for Israel. The twelve tribes have not been written off by God. Twelve thousand from each tribe will be sealed by the Holy Spirit. The number is symbolic. It anticipates the day when "all Israel shall be saved," as the apostle Paul puts it in Romans 11:25.

However, revival will not touch the Jewish race alone. Verses 9–10 widen our horizons, and draw our attention to all nations, from which a multitude too numerous to calculate will praise God for his salvation. The chapter ends (verses 13–17) by extolling the justified standing of God's people, seen in their robes made white by the blood of Christ, and by portraying their total satisfaction and unmitigated joy. These are the marks of revived believers, even in a world where they face tribulation.

THE CHURCH IN THE WORLD: PREACHING, SUFFERING, PRAYING FOR REVIVAL (REVELATION 8:1–11:14)

The seventh seal (Revelation 8:1–6) serves as an introduction to the seven trumpets. They have a familiar ring. The experiences denoted by the seals reappear. This emphasizes the all-pervading reality of such experiences in the course of the history of this fallen world. The first four trumpets occur in quick succession (Revelation 8:7–12). They portray natural disasters on land, at sea, and in the air. They illustrate such things as earthquakes, pollution and hijackings. However, the fact that these things are associated with trumpets is significant. We are reminded of Ezekiel 33:3–6, where trumpets serve as warnings. The trumpets do not represent final judgment. Their devastation is only one third each time. The disasters contained in the trumpets, disasters which occur through the course of history, have a judgmental aspect, certainly, but they are also warnings of judgment to come.

Revelation 8:3–5 shows that the disasters which occur in history are connected with the prayers of God's people. The thrust of all our praying is that the Lord would save souls through the preaching of the gospel. But God knows better than we do that sometimes, to move people to respond to the gospel and come to Christ, it is necessary to shake them to the depths of their being with warnings of coming judgment. We may not always think of earthquakes, pollution and hijackings as God's answers to our prayers. But perhaps they are. We pray for revival, and God may multiply disasters in order to rock people out of their complacency and lethargy, to alert them to their danger, and so prepare them to hear and receive his word. Better is short-lived pain now and then eternal joy, than a lifetime of fun followed by eternal misery.

When we come to Revelation 8:13 an ominous note is sounded. Each of the remaining three trumpets has a "Woe" attached to it. These three trumpets have a more sinister feel. The descriptions are more intense. We realize that we are not now talking about ordinary disasters. Now all hell is let loose on earth. Here is a challenge to take the warnings of judgment seriously, a resounding insistence that the consequences of ignoring the warnings are truly terrible.

The fifth trumpet (Revelation 9:1–12) is a locust plague. Yet the locusts are not intended to be taken literally. Literal locusts eat nothing but vegetation, whereas these leave the vegetation alone (verse 4). Literal locusts do not sting, as these do (verse 5); they bite. The shape and sound of these locusts are both abnormal (verses 7–9). What is more, these locusts emerge out of the darkness and smoke of the pit (verses 2–3). So they are symbolic of sinister forces of evil at work in the world. They remind us that demonic powers are real, that they torment people and drive them to despair (verses 5–6). Their total aim is to destroy men and women: the names "Abaddon" and "Apollyon" (verse 11) mean "destruction" and "destroyer" respectively. However, verse 3 insists that these demonic forces have been "given power." Verse 5 says that their tormenting ability was "granted to them," but it was limited: they had to stop short of killing. The power of demons is not intrinsic to themselves. They can only operate to the extent that God permits, and sometimes God employs demonic powers in sounding forth the warnings of his wrath to come, though God always protects his church (verse 4).

The sixth trumpet (Revelation 9:13–21) depicts a symbolic army: two hundred million men on horseback would be impossible to conscript, transport and supply literally. The point of this trumpet is to reiterate that God is at work in the disasters of history, warning of judgment to come, and working out his present judgment in the world. That is why there is an echo of the judgment on Sodom and Gomorrah, with the references to fire and brimstone (verses 17–18; cf. Genesis 19:24).

However, embedded within this sixth trumpet is a passage (Revelation 10:1—11:14) explaining the situation of the church in the world today. Six different images represent the church: John himself (10:8–11), the temple, altar and worshippers (11:1), the holy city (11:2), the two witnesses (11:3), the two olive trees (11:4) and the two lampstands (11:4). In picture language this passage tells us two main things about the church in the contemporary world.

First, the church's task is to preach the gospel. This is summed up in the word "prophesy" (Revelation 10:11; 11:3). The church can only effectively carry through this preaching ministry if it has first imbibed the teaching of God's word, called here "the little book" (10:9–10). This gospel task is carried out with a global vision (10:11): "many peoples, nations, tongues, and kings" means absolutely everywhere. It goes on for the entire age which began with the ascension of Christ (11:3), symbolized as one thousand two hundred and sixty days. Again we are challenged to keep on with the work of the gospel. There must be no let-up to our evangelism.

Second, the church must expect to face persecution. This is a recurrent reality (11:2), though sometimes it may acquire more severe proportions (11:7), even resulting in martyrdom (11:9–10). Once again we must face the challenge: what is our motivation in praying for revival. If it is to avoid persecution we have missed the point.

THE WORLD DECEIVED: YET REVIVAL A CERTAINTY (REVELATION 11:15–14:20)

That Revelation is not intended to be a chronological account of Christian history is clear from the opening verses of the passage about the seventh trumpet. First we are given a preview of God's ultimate goal, the transfer of world government to Christ (Revelation 11:15–21), and then we have a flashback which sets that ultimate goal in context (Revelation 12:1–5). It reiterates the point that the end really began with the first coming of Christ. For, of course, the government of the world has belonged to Christ ever since his ascension. But for the time being the devil has been allowed to usurp authority (cf. Luke 4:5–6). However, a time is coming when the Lord will reclaim his possession, take his great power and reign.

With the seventh trumpet our attention has already been directed towards the final part of this period of history (Revelation 10:7). However, we are led gradually to the climactic era.

The ascension of Christ is described in symbolic terms in Revelation 12:5. The main result, as far as this passage is concerned, is that Satan was thrown out of heaven. His illegal throne was toppled. Now his main activity is to deceive the whole world (verse 9). Knowing that should obviously drive us to prayer that the eyes of deceived people may be opened to see the truth of the gospel.

In a deceived world, God's people face persecution. This is true both for God's ancient people, Israel, and for the church composed of believers from every nation. The woman in Revelation 12 represents Israel. Verse 13 tells of her persecution by the devil. The twentieth-century holocaust was probably the worst example in history of the persecution of the Jews. And yet Israel has been accorded divine protection and preserved (verses 6, 14-16). However, Satan also turns his venom on the church (verse 17). We should not be surprised if part of our Christian calling is suffering.

Chapters 13-14 elaborate on the sufferings of God's people in the present world. Revelation 13:7 picks up the reference to the dragon's war with the church (Revelation 12:17). These chapters are an overview of the entire period since the ascension of Christ. Revelation 13:1-10 introduces us to the beast. It is unwise to try to pinpoint the beast by identifying it with some particular tyrant or tyrannical system. Verse 1 portrays the beast rising out of the sea. Isaiah 57:20 sheds some light on this: the sea represents restless wickedness. The beast symbolizes human power and organization on the basis of restless wickedness. It is a general description of human affairs, political, economic, social, religious, educational, commercial—all rooted in godlessness. There is something beastly about this world as constituted in rebellion against God.

We learn three main things about this beastly system of human ideology. (1) The beast embodies the power of Satan. It resembles the dragon: verse 1 is very similar to the description of the dragon in Revelation 12:3, and it is the dragon who gives the beast its power (verse 2). (2) The beast claims a loyalty which is due only to God. Three times the beast is described as a blasphemer (verses 1, 5, 6), and verse 7 speaks of its authority "over every tribe, tongue, and nation"—a sinister parody of Christ's legitimate authority (cf. Revelation 5:9; 7:9). (3) The beast survives against expectations. It received a deadly wound, and yet, surprisingly, the wound was healed (verses 3, 12, 14). The wound is probably the death-blow struck by Christ against the devil and every expression of his power. However, as yet the beastly power of sinful ideology lives on. Even where the gospel makes its mighty impact, it seems that the power of evil soon gains the ascendancy again. So here is a description of a beastly world in which God's people are the victims of the devil's aggression against God.

At verse 11 a second beast appears on the scene. It is later called "the false prophet" (Revelation 16:13; 19:20). The fact that this beast is described as a false prophet implies that it comes with a message purporting to be the truth, but actually a perpetration of error. It symbolizes the ungodly ideologies which underlie all human power and organization. They may well have a religious aspect, whether false religion such as Islam, or the deliberate irreligion of a multi-faith approach which aims to nullify faith itself. Once again the key word is deception (verse 14). People generally are deceived by the world's brainwashing and indoctrination. Moreover, God's people are ostracized (verse 17).

Chapter 14 now offers a word of encouragement to God's suffering people. Israel is secure in Christ's protection (verses 1–5), and the international church boldly proclaims the gospel. From God's perspective, that is the really significant thing about this present epoch of history. Whenever we are involved in gospel work we are at the very cutting-edge of all that is going on in the world. And a harvest is assured (verses 14–16). We may labor with genuine expectancy and optimism. We are not going to be beaten. Even in a deceived world, revivals are certain to take place. Jesus has won and will win: he won the victory over the devil at the cross, and he will finally drive that victory home in the salvation of the nations of the world. The chapter finishes with a warning of the fate of those who persist in rejecting the gracious invitation of the gospel (verses 17–20).

DECEIVED NO MORE: THE ULTIMATE GLOBAL REVIVAL (REVELATION 15–20)

This section of Revelation anticipates the final victory of the gospel, the ultimate revival, which will unite the entire world under the banner of Jesus Christ. The key characteristic of that time will be the end of deception (Revelation 20:3). This means that it must be a different epoch from any so far described in Revelation, where deception has been the main recurring feature. Revelation 12:9 and 13:14 use the verb "to deceive" in the present tense, describing the permanent reality of that era, whereas Revelation 18:23 and 19:20 look back to that former period, using the verb in the past tense, implying that such a situation exists no more.

The Decisive Victory of the Gospel

In chapters 15 and 16 we have seven bowls, "full of the wrath of God" (15:7), also called "the seven last plagues" in which "the wrath of God is complete." The first three plagues continue themes which we have met earlier in the book. Illness and pollution are still marks of life in this fallen world (Revelation 16:2-4), and the fourth plague sounds a bit like global warming (Revelation 16:8-9). But, as with the trumpets, the later bowls acquire a more sinister hue. The fifth bowl portrays the collapse of government, leading to an atmosphere of darkness throughout the world (Revelation 16:10-11), while the sixth bowl again emphasizes the demonic involvement which unites the world in its battle with God (Revelation 16:12-16). It seems that the intention is to portray the way in which demonic forces are always aiming to achieve global harmony in opposition to Christ and the truth. We are assured that throughout this time the church will remain secure in its Savior (Revelation 15:2-4; 16:5-7).

However, as the seventh bowl is poured out this demonic unity is suddenly shattered. The cry is heard, "It is done!" (Revelation 16:17-20). Here is the full victory of the gospel towards the end of this present age, the ultimate revival.

Chapters 17-19 give more detail about the collapse of the demon-inspired, beastly system of this world. The beast is now seen with a harlot riding on its back. The system is nicknamed "Babylon." The description of the scarlet beast in Revelation 17:3 shows that it is the same beast as the first one of chapter 13 (cf. Revelation 13:1). Every human society worldwide has fallen in love with that all-pervading rebellious spirit. This is the mother ideological principle which gives birth to every varied expression of sin without exception (Revelation 17:2-5). Revelation 17:12 portrays the beastly world system having its final fling in many kingdoms, but, as verse 14 insists, the victory of the Lamb is an absolute certainty.

Chapter 18 describes the collapse of the power of evil, and the victory of Christ as this period of history reaches its climax. Verses 1-3 are a summary, proclaiming the collapse of the devil-inspired system of godlessness and rebellion. Verses 4-20 contain a series of laments as various categories of people see everything that they have lived and worked for collapsing to nothing. At the end of the chapter we have an enacted parable: a huge millstone is thrown into the sea, and sinks without trace. This represents the finality of God's judgment on Babylon (verses 21-24). This leads into chapter 19, where verses 1–10 are a celebration of God's victory in Christ, which is absolutely complete.

A new section begins at Revelation 19:11. The passage which follows depicts the world as it will be following Christ's complete victory. Verses 11–16 portray Christ riding forth to win the world for his kingdom. It is significant that "his name is called The Word of God" (verse 13). I think that is a reminder that it is through the preaching of the gospel that he will win the nations.

Verse 15 contains familiar imagery. We have suggested already that the rod of iron is the gospel message. The Lord strikes the nations with the sword of the Spirit, the Word of the gospel, subdues them to his side, and so rules them by the same gospel. As the king comes in gospel power, so the beast vanishes from the scene (verses 17–21). The evil system of anti-God rebellion is overthrown. The main point is how quick and decisive Christ's ultimate victory will be when it comes. The kings of the earth, united in their allegiance to the beast assemble for war, but no war takes place. Instead, the beast and the false prophet are instantly captured. At God's appointed time the godless system of rebellion which dominates the thinking and practices of the world will be consigned to oblivion in a moment.

Reigning with Christ

It seems that the so-called "millennium" of Revelation 20 is a pictorial account of the fresh era of world history which will then follow. It is the final promised age of global revival. I assume that the one thousand years is a symbolic number. We cannot say how long this era of peace and justice and gospel triumph will last.

I understand the structure of this passage as follows: verses 1–4a are a summary, and verses 4b–15 then fill in the details. The summary falls into three parts: (1) Satan will be bound for the thousand years, so ending deception (verses 1–3a); (2) Satan will be released after the thousand years for a little while (verse 3b); (3) the final judgment takes place (verse 4a).

Verses 4b–6 amplify verses 1–3a. They add the information that the saints will reign with Christ for the thousand years. Verses 7–10 amplify verse 3b. They inform us that, at the end of the thousand years, Satan will be released. The nations will be deceived again. The church will face renewed persecution, but God will intervene and finalize his victory as the devil is despatched to his eternal doom. Verses 11–15 amplify verse 4a. The final event of history will be the judgment.

GLOBAL REVIVAL—AND ON TO GLORY (REVELATION 21-22)

It is a moot point whether chapters 21 and 22 continue the story beyond the judgment, or whether they are another flashback, filling out yet more of the details of what life will be like on earth during that period after the gospel has finally conquered all nations, and the reign of Christ is evident on earth before the end. Matthew Henry[5] and Matthew Poole[6] each point out that both views were around in their days. Amongst more recent commentators George Beasley-Murray[7] and Terry Brooks[8] both read at least part of these chapters as descriptive of the blessings of the millennial age, the fruits of global revival. Perhaps it is not necessary to make an absolute choice between these two possibilities. The glories of the eternal state will surely cast their light back into time, especially when the gospel has triumphed worldwide. The difference will be one of degree, not one of kind.

Nevertheless, for our present purpose it is relevant to read these chapters as a fuller description than we have in chapter 20 of the blessings of the millennial age, when the gospel has triumphed worldwide. And there is good reason to understand these chapters as referring to the impact of the gospel in the present age. The nations are mentioned three times—in Revelation 21:24, 21:26, and 22:2. This in itself implies that the final period of this present history is at least partly in view: there will presumably be no distinction of nations in the eternal state. Moreover, the last of these references speaks of "the healing of the nations." There will surely be no need of healing once the ultimate state of eternal glory has begun. It seems then that these chapters are designed to give us a glimpse of what life on earth will be like in that final period, once global revival has taken place, once the gospel has triumphed everywhere.

The dominant feature of that period will be the manifest reality of God dwelling with the human race. This is stated in Revelation 21:3, and illustrated in verses 9–22. This reality will be experienced subjectively as

5. Henry, *New Testament*, Vol. 10, 289.

6. Poole, *New Testament*, 1004.

7. Beasley-Murray, "Revelation," 1305; ibid., *Book of Revelation*, 315–18.

8. Brooks, *Revelation*, 122–23.

unmitigated joy (Revelation 21:4) and unlimited satisfaction (Revelation 21:6). Its results will be twofold. First, the life of the nations worldwide will be totally transformed, such that every nation will walk in the light of gospel truth, and bring to the living God and to Jesus Christ the glory and honor which is his due (Revelation 21:24–26). Second, the visible church on earth will be totally purified. Liberal theology will be dead and gone. Nominalism will be rooted out. All Christians will live in radical obedience and perfect service, in deep fellowship with God (Revelation 21:27; 22:3–4).

Verse 24 refers to the kings glorifying God. It is a recurrent Old Testament emphasis, especially in the books of Psalms and Isaiah, that kings and princes will bow before the true king of kings. For example, Psalm 72:11 specifies that all the kings of the world will fall down before Christ as the nations serve him. Isaiah 49:7 says that kings and princes will worship Christ.[9] Here is the description of the day when all those prophecies come to their fulfillment.

This gives us a strong mandate to pray for the leaders of the world. We must pray that monarchs, presidents, and prime ministers will be brought to their knees before Jesus Christ, acknowledging that he is their Lord, so that they tremble at the very idea of passing any legislation that conflicts with the word of God. In the final era of global revival, the leadership of every nation will openly recognize that Jesus Christ is king and that the one, true, living God is the Lord of all the earth. All political power in that day will be shaped by Christian truth. As we anticipate such a day with real excitement, it is our privilege to participate by prayer in God's purpose which is working towards that goal.

Other aspects of that coming age of gospel glory will be remarkable productivity and national healing: poverty, injustice, war will be things of the past, as the curse on the earth will be canceled, and the light of divine glory will pervade the entire cultural atmosphere (Revelation 22:2–3, 5). Then, as Revelation 22:7 indicates, after Satan's brief release (Revelation 20:3, 7), all that remains is for Christ to come, and translate the millennial age into the eternal kingdom of heavenly glory.

9. See also Pss 2:10; 47:9; 102:15; 138:4; 148:11; Isa 32:1; 60:11; 62:2.

6

CONCLUSION

Revival a New Testament Theme

We have completed our voyage of discovery through the pages of the
New Testament. The conclusion which has been constantly indicated as we have traveled is that, while the exact word "revival" may be absent,
the reality of revival is definitely a New Testament theme, and therefore that
prayer for revival has a clear New Testament mandate, and so is an obligation for Christian people today and at any time.

In response to those who protest that revival is an Old Testament concept, which finds its total fulfillment in the coming of Christ, we acknowledge that there is truth in this claim, but that the fulfillment is not limited
to the life, death, resurrection, and ascension of Jesus, and the initial outpouring of the Holy Spirit at Pentecost consequent upon Christ's glorification. The New Testament portrays a phenomenon of church life and gospel
success from which we in Yorkshire, the rest of the UK, the western world
in general, and many other parts of the globe, are, at present, far removed.

This must challenge us, if we genuinely believe that Scripture is normative. We dare not classify the New Testament experience as extraordinary,
and settle for a lower level of spiritual life, which we presume to label "ordinary." To do that is to borrow the methodology of liberal theology, which
explains away the teaching of Scripture in the light of our experience. A
proper biblical methodology adopts the reverse approach: it feels the far-
reaching challenge of the normative biblical standard, which rebukes the

lackluster spirituality and the ineffectiveness of gospel witness, which mark so much of church life today.

Moreover, the implication in the protest that revival is an Old Testament theme appears to be that we may read the two Testaments in isolation from each other. We have discovered in our studies that the New Testament itself makes such a strategy impossible. From its opening verse onwards the New Testament is constantly drawing upon Old Testament texts, passages, themes, prophecies. We cannot construct a New Testament theology of revival independently of the Old Testament, just because the New Testament consistently pulls Old Testament teaching into its own theology.

This study has resoundingly challenged the despondency which marks so much of the contemporary church. As Bible believers, we should be bursting with expectancy. The promises of God's word hold out to us the prospect of complete gospel success in this present age before the return of Christ. That joyful hope should fuel our prayers, stimulate our service, and uplift our hearts. We are on the victory side. As we have remarked several times, that does not necessarily mean that life will become more comfortable for Christians in this world. God's purpose may be to use persecution as a tool to move his work forward in revival. But like the apostles, if we truly love the Lord, we shall then rejoice in being counted worthy to suffer shame for his name (Acts 5:41).

It is the glory and honor of Jesus which matters. Revival is our Lord Jesus Christ receiving the esteem which is his due, obtaining the reputation on earth which he deserves. And the New Testament expectation is that the Father will keep his promises to his Son, and give him the nations as his inheritance through the preaching of the gospel in the course of this present age.

So, with the Psalmist, we pray, "Revive me, O LORD, for your name's sake!" (Psalm 143:11). With the Levites in Ezra 9:9, we long that God would "revive us" and "repair the house of God." With the apostle Paul, we plead for that day of total gospel victory, that day when Jews and Gentiles the world over are united in the abundant riches of God's reconciling mercy in Christ, that day which can only be described as "life from the dead" (Romans 11:15).

7

POSTSCRIPT

Rise Up, You Heirs of God's Salvation

On a recent teaching trip to the Far East I heard a rousing tune being played by a brass band. On making some enquiries I discovered that it was the tune which Pierre Degeyter set in 1888 to the revolutionary song *The Internationale*. I thought it would be a great tune for rousing God's people to prayer for revival. So I was stimulated to set new words to it. Here is the result.

1. Rise up, you heirs of God's salvation,
Renew devotion to his name;
Set free from hell and condemnation,
Now let his glory be your aim.
Since this world shall be Christ's dominion,
Arouse yourselves to fervent prayer;
Don't fall for negative opinion,
Do not embrace faithless despair.

Refrain
For God's promise, far-reaching,
Gives the world to his Son;
By Spirit-fired preaching
The nations shall be won.

Yes, God's promise, far-reaching,
Gives the world to his Son;
By Spirit-fired preaching
The nations shall be won.

2. Christ Jesus is the only Savior,
On him alone we can depend.
Despite this sinful world's behavior,
Our faith expects a glorious end.
We'll press on, called to gospel labor,
For Christ we'll seek to win the lost;
Filled with his love, we'll love our neighbor,
We'll serve the Lord at any cost.

3. Our Father is the world's Creator:
His Son inherits all he made.
Compared with all things Christ is greater –
His blazing glory cannot fade.
Undeterred by the devil's roarings,
We stand secure in radiant hope;
We pray for mighty, fresh outpourings –
The Spirit's power has global scope!

4. Since God shows mercy and compassion
Towards a world that still rebels,
We pray that we may share his passion,
Lead thirsty souls to living wells.
We await great worldwide revival—
Christ Jesus recognized as Lord;
At last he'll reign without a rival—
This broken world to peace restored.

Words by Jonathan Bayes (2015)
Tune: *The Internationale* by Pierre Degeyter (1888)

BIBLIOGRAPHY

Barnes, Albert. *A Popular Family Commentary on the New Testament, Vol. 3: Acts of the Apostles*. London: Blackie, 1886.

Bayes, Jonathan F. *The Weakness of the Law: God's Law and the Christian in New Testament Perspective*. Paternoster Biblical and Theological Monographs. Carlisle: Paternoster, 2000.

Beasley-Murray, George R. *The Book of Revelation*. London: Oliphants, 1978.

———. "The Revelation." In *The New Bible Commentary Revised*, edited by Donald Guthrie and J. Alec Motyer, 1279–1310. Leicester: IVP, 1970.

Boettner, Lorraine. *The Reformed Doctrine of Predestination*. Phillipsburg: Presbyterian and Reformed, 1932.

Brooks, Terry. *Revelation: Meaningful Mysteries for Today*. Bradford: Harvestime, 1988.

Calvin, John. *Commentaries on the Book of the Prophet Jeremiah and the Lamentations*. 4 vols. 1565. Reprint, Grand Rapids: Baker, 1979.

———. *Commentary upon the Acts of the Apostles*. 2 vols. 1585. Reprint, Grand Rapids: Baker, 1979.

Cauchi, Tony. *Revivals in the New Testament*. Revival Library, 2009. www.revival-library. org/pensketches/revivals/03nt.html.

Coenen, Lothar. "*kērussō.*" In *New International Dictionary of New Testament Theology, Vol. 3*, edited by Colin Brown, 48–57. Exeter: Paternoster, 1971.

France, Richard T. *Matthew*. Leicester: IVP, 1985.

Harrell, David E. *All Things are Possible: the Healing and Charismatic Revivals in Modern America*. Bloomington: Indiana University Press, 1975.

Harris, R. Laird, et al. *Theological Wordbook of the Old Testament*. Carluke: Online Bible Edition, 1987–2011.

Hendriksen, William. *Matthew*. Edinburgh: Banner of Truth, 1974.

Henry, Matthew. *An Exposition of the New Testament*. 10 vols. 1712. Reprint, London: Mackenzie, 1870.

Hodge, Charles. *Systematic Theology*. 3 vols. London: Nelson, 1880.

Marsden, George M. *Jonathan Edwards: A Life*. New Haven: Yale University Press, 2003.

Moore, Thomas V. *Zechariah*. 1856. Reprint, Edinburgh: Banner of Truth, 1958.

Motyer, J. Alec. *The Prophecy of Isaiah*. Leicester: IVP, 1993.

Passantino, Robert, and Gretchen Passantino. *The Gates of Hell*. Answers in Action, 2003. http://www.answers.org/bible/gatesofhell.html.

Poole, Matthew. *A Commentary on the Holy Bible, Vol. 3: The New Testament*. 1685, Reprint, Edinburgh: Banner of Truth, 1963.

Rashi. *Complete Tanach with Rashi.* CD-Rom. Chicago: Davka Corporation and Judaica Press, 1999.

Robertson, Archibald Thomas. *Word Pictures of the New Testament.* Broadman, 1932–1933. Carluke: Online Bible Edition, 1987–2011.

Shedd, William G. T. "The Westminster Standards and the 'Larger Hope.'" In *Calvinism: Pure and Mixed,* 116–31. 1893. Reprint, Edinburgh: Banner of Truth, 1986.

Spurgeon, Charles Haddon. "Heavenly Worship." 1856. In *Treasury of the New Testament,* Vol. 4, 783–8. Reprint, London: Marshall, Morgan and Scott, 1934.

Strom, Andrew. *Todd Bentley and the Lakeland Outpouring—a False Healing Revival in Florida.* www.revivalschool.com/florida.html.

Warfield, Benjamin Breckinridge. "Predestination." In *Biblical Doctrines,* 3–67. 1929. Reprint, Edinburgh: Banner of Truth, 1988.

———. *Studies in Tertullian and Augustine.* 1930. Reprint, Westport: Greenwood, 1970.

SCRIPTURE INDEX

OLD TESTAMENT

Genesis

1:26, 28	51
12:1–3	11
13:15	18
17:6	73
18:18	11
19:24	132
22:2, 12, 16	17
22:18	11, 18
26:3–4	18
26:4	11
28:14	12
49:9–10	128

Exodus

4:20	51
7:10–12	52
9:18, 23	52
15:6	36n18
17:9	51
17:9–13	52
35:29	53
36:3	53

Numbers

16:46	36n18
17:1–8	52
24:17	36n18

Deuteronomy

16:10	53
28:33	36n18
32:43	102, 103
33:25	124n2

Joshua

10:24	51
17:18	124n2

2 Samuel

12:15	36n18
22:1, 50	102

1 Kings

9:11	19

1 Chronicles

16:31	76
17:11–14	6
17:13	116
29:11	116

2 Chronicles

6:24	36n18
20:37	36n18

Ezra

9:8–9	3n2
9:9	141

Job

20:19	36n18

Psalms

2	72–76, 116
2:7	77
2:7–8	113
2:9	124
2:10	139n9
8	50
8:6–8	105–6
18	102
22	54–56
33:12	12
45	21
45:6–7	116
45:6	124
47:9	139n9
67:4	76
71:20	3n2
72	8–9
72:11	139
72:18	61
80:18	3n2
85:6	3n2
89	6–8
96:11	76
97:1	76
97:1–9	116–17
98:4	76
100:1–2	76
102	117–18
102:15	139n9
110:1–3	50–54, 72, 105–6
110:1	114
117:1	103
118:22–23	48
118:25–26	46–48
119:25, 37, 40, 88, 107, 149, 154, 156, 159	3n2
132	9–10

138:4	139n9
138:7	3n2
143:11	3n2, 141
148:1	48
148:11	139n9

Isaiah

2:4	109
2:10, 19, 21	36n18
6:8	13
9:1–7	19–20
9:2	19n7, 31
9:5	13
11:9–10	103
19:24–25	12
22:22	127
29:9–12	31
29:17–18	31–32
32:1	139n9
32:15–20	32
35:4–10	32–33
40:3–8	13–14
42	33–35
42:8	65
44:3	32
48:11	65
49:6–7	78–79
49:7	139
53:4—54:3	29–30
54:4	42
55:3–5	77
56:3–8	49–50
57:15	3n2
57:20	134
58:6	36
59:20–21	98
60:11	139n9
61	35–36
62:2	139n9

Jeremiah

7:11	49
23:5–6	10
33:6–9, 15–17	10–11
51:30	36n18

Lamentations

1:1	42

Ezekiel

20:37	124
21:7, 15	36n18
33:3-6	131

Daniel

2:40, 42	124n2
2:44	21
7:13-14, 27	21
7:7	124n2

Hosea

14:7	3n2

Joel

2:28-32	85-87

3:3	86n6

Amos

9:11-12	79

Micah

4:3	109

Habakkuk

1:5—2:14	77-78
2:14	103
3:2	3n2

Zechariah

9	44-46

Malachi

3-4	14

NEW TESTAMENT

Matthew

1:1	5-12, 47n25
1:17	109
1:20	47n25
2:6	124n1
3:3	13
3:5-7	14-15
3:10-12	16
3:14	17
3:17	17
4:3-9	18
4:12-17	19
4:24-25	26
5:22	16n4
6:10	21
6:32-33	21-22
7:19	16n4
8:1, 18	26n9
8:1, 5, 10-11	26-27
8:16-18	29-30
8:16	27n10
9:10	27n11
9:27	47n25
9:36-38	28
11:2-5	30-31
11:10	14
12:15	26n9
12:17-21	33-34
12:23	47n25
13:2	26n9
13:31-33	22
13:40	16n4
14:14	26n9
14:36	27n12
15:22	47n25
15:30, 33	26n9
15:30	27n12
16:15-16, 18-19, 21	36-40
16:28	22

Matthew (continued)

17:5	17
18:8–9	16n4
19:2	26n9
20:16	27
20:28	27
20:29	26n9
20:30–31	47n25
21:5	44
21:8	26n9
21:9	46–48, 47n25
21:13, 15–16	49–50
21:15	47n25
21:42	48
22:9–10	27
22:14	27
22:41–46	50–51, 72
22:42	47n25
24:1–26	23–25
24:29	86
25:41	16n4
26:28	27
27:11, 29, 37, 42	25n8
27:35, 39–43, 46	54
28:18–20	57–59

Mark

1:1–3	13–14
1:4–5	14–15
1:7–8	16
1:11	17
1:14–15	19–21
1:33, 37	26
1:34	27n10, 27n12
2:15	27n11
3:7–8	26n9
3:10	27n12
4:1	26n9
5:21, 24	26n9
6:13, 56	27n12
6:34	26n9
8:1	26n9
8:30–32	22
9:1	22
9:7	17
9:43, 48	16n4

9:49	16n5
10:45	27
10:46	26n9
10:47–48	47n26
11:9–10	46–47
11:17	49–50
12:10	48
12:35–37	51, 72
12:35	47n26
13:1–23	23
13:24–25	86
14:24	27
15:2, 9, 12, 18, 26, 32	25n8
15:24	54
15:28	30
15:29–32	54
15:34	54
16:15	56–57

Luke

1:32–33	6n1
1:55, 73	6n1
1:79	19n7
2:4, 11	6n1
2:14	48
3:3	15
3:4–6	13
3:7	15
3:9	16
3:16	16
3:17	16
3:22	17
3:31	47n26
4:3–9	18
4:5–6	133
4:16–21	35
4:26–27	36
4:41	27n10
5:15	26n9
6:17–18	45
6:17	26n9
6:39	36
7:21	27n10, 27n12
8:4	26n9
9:27	22
9:35	17
9:37	26n9

11:2	21
11:5–13	41–42
11:52	40
12:1	26
12:29–31	21–22
13:18–21	22
13:28–29	27
14:16–24	25–26
14:25	26n9
16:23–24	37
17:7	124n1
18:1–8	42–44
18:38–39	47n26
19:38	46–49
19:46	49
20:17	48
20:41–44	52, 72
20:41	47n26
20:47	42
21:5–24	23
22:37	30
23:2–3, 37–38	25n8
23:27	26n9
23:34–37	54
24:27	5
24:39–40	55
24:47	56–57
24:48	24

John

1:23	13
1:33	16
4:35	28
4:38	28
4:39, 41	27n13
6:2, 5	26n9
12:13	46–48
12:15	44
15:6	16n4
16:14	82
17:4	113
18:33, 36–37, 39	25n8
18:36	25
19:3, 12, 14–15, 19, 21	25n8
19:23–24	54
19:28	55
19:30	54, 55, 114

19:31–33	54
19:34, 37	55
19:34	54
19:36	55
20:20	55
20:25	55
21:6	124n1

Acts

1:3–8	69
1:4–5	80
1:5	16
1:8	24, 53, 79
1:14	81
2	80–85
2:3	16
2:4	89
2:16–21	85–87
2:30	72
2:33	88
2:34–35	72
2:34	51
2:36	17, 87
2:41	17, 62
2:47	62
3–4	62–63, 89
3:15	74
3:16, 19	72
3:24	72, 73
3:25–26	72–73
4	68
4:24–33	89–91
4:25–30	72–76
5	90, 91–92
5:14	63
5:41	141
6:1, 7	63
6:3, 5, 8, 10, 15	114
7:55–56	114
8	64–65
8:1, 4	92
8:5, 12	70
8:8	76
8:25	92
9:1–19	65–66
9:20, 27	93
9:31	65

Acts (continued)

9:42	66
10	87–88
10:44	17, 80
11:15–17	88–89
11:16–17	16–17
11:19–20	92
11:21, 24	66
12:24	66
13:16–47	77–79
13:33	74, 113
13:42, 44–45, 49	66
14:1	66
14:7	93
14:21	66
14:22	70
15:16–17	79
16:5	66
16:10	93
17:4, 6	67
17:7	71
17:12	67
18:8, 10	67
19:8	70
19:10, 17, 20, 26	67–68
20:16	68
20:25	70
20:28	124n1
21:20	68, 68n2
28:23, 31	70
28:28	69
28:31	93

Romans

1–8	94
2:14, 19	34
4:13	100–101
5:14	106
5:18–20	101
6:9	77
7:9	2n1
9:2	95
10:1	95
11	94–100, 102
11:15	141
11:25	131

15:8–12	102–4

1 Corinthians

3:11	37
3:13, 15	16n4
4:7	125
13:12	71
15:22–27	104–7
15:24	23

2 Corinthians

4:4	38
10:3–5	39–40

Galatians

1:23	66
3:16	100
4:4	108–9

Ephesians

1:9–10	108–10
2:20	37

Philippians

2:9–11	110–11

Colossians

1:18–20	111–12
2:15	128

1 Thessalonians

1:4–5	112–13
1:5	53

2 Thessalonians

1:8	16n4

Hebrews

1:2–3	113

1:3	116
1:5–12	116–17
1:13	114, 116
2:5–9	50
2:8–9	105
10:11–13	113–14
10:27	16n4
12:22	53
12:29	16n4

James

2:13	29

1 Peter

1:7	16n5
5:2	124n1
5:8	42

2 Peter

3:7	16n4

1 John

3:8	128

Revelation

1	120–21
1:7	55
2–3	121–27
2:7	121
4–5	127–29
4:5	16
5:9	134
6–7	129–31
7:9	27, 134
7:17	124
8:1—11:14	131–33
10:7	133
11:15—14:20	133–35
12:9	135
13:1	136
13:14	135
15–20	135–38
16:13	135
19:20	135
20:3, 7	139
21–22	138–39

Lightning Source UK Ltd.
Milton Keynes UK
UKOW06f2352240316

270866UK00001B/27/P